Skills Training for Tomorrow's Work Force

Skills Training for Tomorrow's Work Force

Laurie Field

Amsterdam • Johannesburg • Oxford
San Diego • Sydney • Toronto

Copyright © 1994 by Pfeiffer & Company
ISBN: 0-88390-433-0

Library of Congress Catalog Card Number: 94-066915
All rights reserved

Printed in the United States of America

Published by Pfeiffer & Company
8517 Production Avenue
San Diego, California 92121
United States of America
1-619-578-5900, FAX 1-619-578-2042

This book is printed on acid-free, recycled stock that meets
or exceeds the minimum GPO and EPA specifications
for recycled paper.

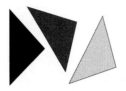

Table of Contents

♦ **Introduction** 1

♦ **Chapter 1: The Need for New Skills** 5
   Organizational Technoculture 5
   Skills in Short Supply 16
   The Social Context of Skills 20

♦ **Chapter 2: The Terminology of Skill Formation** . . 27
   Jobs and Skills 28
   Terms Associated with Jobs 29
   The Nature of Skill 32
   Types of Skills 33
   The Relationship Between Jobs and
      Employees' Skills 42

♦ **Chapter 3: Challenges for Trainers** 47
   Seven Challenges for Trainers 47

♦ **Chapter 4: Investigate Skills and Training Issues** . . 59
   Types of Workplace Research 60
   Collect Occupational Data 61
   Carry Out an Exploratory Study 62

Analyze Training Needs 65
Analyze Tasks 74

♦ **Chapter 5: Analyze Job Competencies** 81
Competency-Based Training Program 81
Advantages and Limitations of Competency-Based
 Training 86
Setting Up a Competency-Based Training Program . . . 88

♦ **Chapter 6: State Performance Objectives** 97
Stating Performance Objectives 98
Uses and Limitations of Performance Objectives . . . 101
Hints for Writing Useful Performance Objectives . . . 103

♦ **Chapter 7: Design and Use Job Aids** 107
Is a Job Aid Needed? 107
Job-Reference Guides 109
Technical-User Manuals 112
On-Line Job Aids 118

♦ **Chapter 8: Structure a Training Program** 125
The Structure of Skills Training 127
Combining Explanations, Demonstrations,
 and Practice 130
Analysis of Competency Patterns 134
Training Employees to Operate Complex
 Integrating Technologies 137
General Approaches to Skills Training 139
Transfer of Skills to the Job 143

♦ **Chapter 9: Train On-the-Job** 147
   Conducting On-the-Job Training 148
   Encouraging Learning at the Workplace 157

♦ **Chapter 10: Use Computers in Training** 163
   Computers in Training 164
   Computer-Managed Learning 170
   Merits of Computer-Based Learning 173
   Computers and Interactive Video 180
   Resistance to Computer-Based Training 184

♦ **Chapter 11: Modular Training** 189
   Modules and Modular Programs 190
   Self-Paced Modules 193
   Learner Guides 196
   Introducing Modular Training 200

♦ **Chapter 12: Explaining and Demonstrating a Task** 203
   Purpose of Combining Explanation and
      Demonstration 204
   Adult Learning and the Demonstration Session 205
   Preparing for the Session 210
   Conducting the Session 212
   Planning the Session 215

♦ **Chapter 13: Supervise Practice** 219
   Structuring Practice 220
   Principles of Practical Instruction 224
   Preparing Practical Notes 232

♦ **Chapter 14: Assess Skills** 235
  Norm-Referenced and Criterion-Referenced Tests . . 236
  Characteristics of an Effective Competency Test . . . 239
  The Process of Skills Assessments 244
  Selecting a Sample of Competencies or Skills 244
  Assessing Skills and Knowledge 246
  Deciding Assessment Results 250

♦ **Index** 259

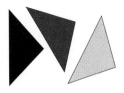

Introduction

There is currently a shortage of workers with the skills needed to support modern industries. It is not simply that workers have too few skills, but that the mix of skills that workers do have is inappropriate. In many cases, groups of workers are highly skilled in areas that are no longer relevant, but lack the skills needed to support the upgrading that is occurring in manufacturing and service industries.

This book reviews all the main aspects of planning, conducting, and assessing training in job-related skills. Chapter 1, *The Need for New Skills*, examines four main technocultural factors that affect industry training and learning: industrial relations, technology, work organization, and skill formation. The chapter explores each of the four factors in an attempt to explain why there is such a need to provide new skills for workers.

Chapter 2, *The Terminology of Skill Formation*, defines "skill" and explains the skills-iceberg model. The definitions in this chapter provide a foundation for the rest of the book. Chapter 3, *Challenges for Trainers*, presents seven problematic issues that trainers will have to grapple with to be successful. Chapter 4, *Investigate Skills and Training Issues*, discusses action research and more formal approaches to studying workplace issues.

Chapter 5, *Analyze Job Competencies*, covers some of the features of competency-based training. It describes the characteristics of this training approach and looks at its advantages and disadvantages. The chapter also discusses the steps involved in setting up a competency-based training program.

Chapter 6, *State Performance Objectives*, looks at performance objectives and discusses the correct way to word them. It examines their applications and limitations and provides a number of suggestions for writing and using performance objectives effectively.

Chapter 7, *Design and Use Job Aids*, examines factors that determine whether job aids are needed to support skilled work. The chapter also provides three examples of the most common types of job aids.

Chapter 8, *Structure a Training Program*, looks at some of the factors that influence the sequence and structure of individual training sessions and training programs.

Chapter 9, *Train on the Job*, deals with job training and learning. The chapter discusses the broader issue of workplace learning, and suggests ways in which the worksite can become a place where learning and skill development are encouraged.

Chapter 10, *Use Computers in Training*, provides an overview of computer-based training. The chapter defines terminology and outlines factors that need to be considered when deciding whether computer-based training is appropriate.

Chapter 11, *Modular Training*, discusses self-paced modular programs. The chapter also discusses the format of learner guides, which are often provided for each module. In addition, it offers some suggestions regarding the introduction of modular training.

Chapter 12, *Explaining and Demonstrating a Task*, covers the basic techniques of combining explanations with hands-on demonstrations within a training session. The chapter explains how to write and structure a lesson plan for a session which combines explanation with demonstration.

Chapter 13, *Supervise Practice*, looks at the stages that are typically involved in practical supervision. The chapter then examines in detail the psychology of practice and suggests ways that learning can be encouraged.

Chapter 14, *Assess Skills*, looks at what is known about assessing work skills and competencies. The chapter examines the purpose of assessment and discusses the stages in developing assessment materials that are concerned with skill development.

Employees have a dominant role in controlling technology and day-to-day operations

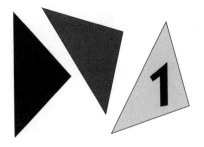

The Need for New Skills

Skill formation has been neglected by organizations for many years. It is a holistic concept that includes education, personal development, formal vocational training, on-the-job learning, and experiential learning.

The result of neglecting skill-formation policies and practices is that there is currently a shortage of skilled employees who can support modern industries. It is not simply that employees have too few skills—although in some industries that is the case—but that employees have an inappropriate mix of skills. In many cases, groups of employees are highly skilled in areas that are obsolete, but they lack the skills necessary to support the upgrading that is occurring in manufacturing and service industries.

Organizational Technoculture

One person who has contributed greatly to surfacing this problem is Professor Bill Ford from the University of New South Wales. Professor Ford has long been an advocate of reform in approaches to skill formation and a critic of fragmented systems of skills training.

Professor Ford's view, which is echoed in this book, is that reform will be successful only if the complexity of the process of skill formation is recognized and its links to organizational technoculture are understood. (The term *technoculture*[1] refers to the patterns of relationships between technology and the social system.)

Professor Ford has developed a series of diagrams that demonstrate of the links between training, learning, and other aspects of organizational technoculture. Figure 1.1, which is an adaptation of one such diagram, shows some of the main technoculture factors that affect industry training and learning:

- Industrial relations
- Technology
- Work organization
- Skill formation

Figure 1.1. The Main Technoculture Factors That Affect Skill Training and Learning[2]

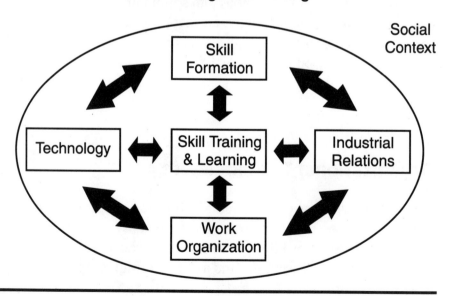

Figure 1.1 also makes reference to social context as an important factor in understanding the nature of skills.

This chapter explores each of the four factors in an attempt to explain why there is a need to provide employees with new skills.

Industrial Relations

Debate in this area has been primarily concerned with the policies and processes of restructuring, such as the issue of whether the focus should be at the enterprise level or across whole industries.

The various parties to industrial relations have differing expectations of the outcomes of restructuring the workplace. Expectations lie somewhere along a continuum that goes from "more money with little or no change" to "more productive forms of work organization and management" (Figure 1.2). What motivates many of those who are pressing for reform at the moment is the hope of achieving the latter.

A number of specific reforms have been advocated. Those that have a direct bearing on skill formation include:

- Removing obsolete job classifications;
- Rewriting job descriptions to broaden the range of competencies that employees could be required to perform;
- Establishing skill-related career paths that link training, skills, and wages and provide ongoing incentives for employees to be involved in skill formation.

Technology

Technological transfer and technological change are two closely related factors that have contributed to present demands for a more highly skilled work force. New technology has had an

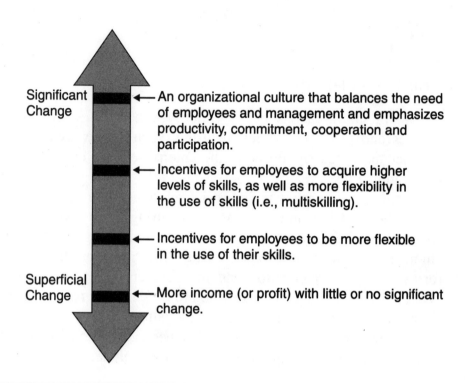

Figure 1.2. Different Agendas for Restructuring the Workplace [3]

Significant Change
- An organizational culture that balances the need of employees and management and emphasizes productivity, commitment, cooperation and participation.
- Incentives for employees to acquire higher levels of skills, as well as more flexibility in the use of skills (i.e., multiskilling).
- Incentives for employees to be more flexible in the use of their skills.

Superficial Change
- More income (or profit) with little or no significant change.

influence on virtually every aspect of work. Following are two examples:

* In the product and service industries, such as retail stores, airline-reservation offices, and financial institutions, there has been a dramatic shift from traditional paperwork to work done on electronic systems such as word processors, data-input terminals that feed into on-line transaction systems, and personal computers.

* In the manufacturing industries, microelectronics has paved the way for changes in production systems. Flex-

ible manufacturing systems (FMS), computer-aided design (CAD), computer-aided manufacture (CAM), and robotics have been introduced widely. Sophisticated computer systems that integrate manufacturing processes with administrative-control processes (computer-integrated manufacturing or CIM) have been developed recently and are likely to have a significant impact on work in many organizations.

An organization's future will depend on how well it adapts to technologies such as these. The key issue here is integration. It is not enough for organizations to import the latest equipment and systems and simply install them, as has often happened. What is called for is an integrated approach to upgrading that recognizes that new technology cannot be treated in isolation from other aspects of organizational technoculture.

The computer-integrated systems that are used in data management, manufacturing, and processing industries offer important implications and challenges for skills training:

- Computer systems have become increasingly complex, interdependent, and expensive;
- Computer systems often require a multidisciplinary approach to both operation and maintenance;
- Fewer employees are needed per unit of output;
- Outputs are very reliant on the operator's level of skill and knowledge;
- Production-process malfunctions or use of incorrect data can have costly consequences;
- Customers' quality-control specifications are becoming increasingly strict;
- Circuits are integrated and are often "intelligent";

- It has become harder for employees to understand how individual system components work and interact; and

- A greater proportion of employees' time is spent dealing with situations that are complex and occur infrequently.

Work Organization

The culture of many organizations has traditionally been characterized by adversarial management-employee relations and stringent management-control mechanisms reminiscent of the ideas of Frederic Taylor. Taylor argued that the thinking and planning associated with work should be handled by management and that employees should be encouraged to do management's bidding through a system of incentives. Taylor's work practices are characterized by the fragmentation of jobs, the provision of individual incentives so that cooperative group work is discouraged, and the removal of employee control over output.

It has become increasingly obvious that Taylorist work practices are not an appropriate basis for today's organization of work and employees. A goal that has been attracting a lot of attention recently is the development of more cooperative, participative relations between employees and managers.

The achievement of such a goal requires changes in job design, management structures and systems, and management-employee relations. Some of the characteristics of organizations that have achieved more cooperative relations and greater employee commitment are shown in Figure 1.3. Both technology and industrial relations matters have contributed to the need for these types of changes. Modern technologies are best suited to organizations in which the following conditions exist:

- Employees are organized into groups that are responsible for their own outputs;

Figure 1.3. Suggested Changes in Organizations That Lead to More Cooperative Relations [4]

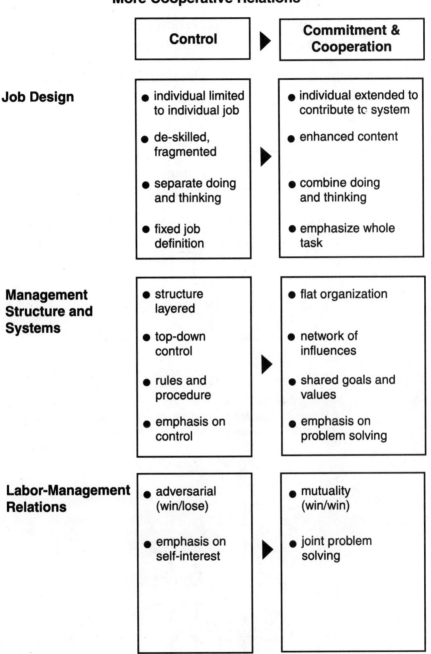

The Need for New Skills

- As many product-related activities as possible are carried out within a production area; and
- There is minimal specialization among the employees and groups interacting within the system.

Hierarchical organizations with rigid lines of authority and impermeable demarcation barriers are incompatible with many modern technologies (Figure 1.4).

Figure 1.4. The Relationship Between Methods of Production and Work Organization [5]

It makes little sense for work processes to be planned this way:

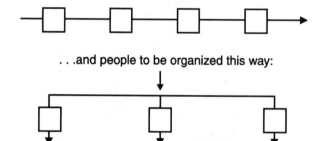

...and people to be organized this way:

...When information or products move among machines or system components this way:

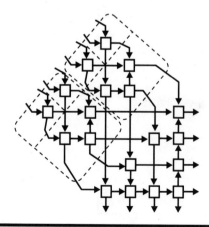

Industrial-relations matters also help to account for current pressures to foster more cooperative work relations. The industrial-relations framework has traditionally given little emphasis to work relations, and work has often been hampered by demarcations, overstaffing, and fragmented jobs. These problems, when combined with the economic downturns of the 80s and 90s, have set the scene for all the parties to industrial relations to devise ways of organizing work more effectively.

Skill Formation

The concept of *skill* is not very well understood, although this is not often acknowledged in the training and labor-relations literature. Skill can refer to any of the behaviors or abilities that an individual has, such as *conceptual skill* or *verbal skill*. A conventional approach is to classify skills into one of the following three types:

- Cognitive (thinking or knowing)
- Perceptual (sensing)
- Psychomotor (doing)

This approach to classifying skills is useful in some types of training, especially in industries in which work mainly involves routine, hands-on tasks. Figure 1.5 shows how this approach to classifying skills can be applied to the work of a cabinetmaker.

In many types of work, however, the thinking/sensing/doing classification is hard to apply. In particular, it is not well suited to the analysis of skills used by employees who operate complex, integrated computer systems such as those found in many service, manufacturing, and processing industries.

An alternative approach to understanding the nature of work skills is the "skills-iceberg" model. This model, which is discussed in Chapter 2, likens an individual's skills to an iceberg and distinguishes between the following types of skills:

* Skills that are used to do routine tasks. In terms of the skills-iceberg model, these are "above the surface." Skills that could be labeled as "above the surface" include typing a letter or processing an application form.

* Skills that are intangible, difficult to observe, and nonroutine. In terms of the skills-iceberg model, these are

Figure 1.5. Cognitive, Perceptual, and Psychomotor Skills Involved in Cabinetmaking

Type of Skill		Example
• *Cognitive* skills involve understanding and using symbols and language.		Reading and interpreting a plan is a cognitive skill.
• *Perceptual* skills involve the use of the senses (sight, feel, etc). They include the ability to estimate distances, recognize angles, and respond to various cues.		Judging whether an angle is correct is a perceptual skill.
• *Psychomotor* skills involve the use of movement of some parts of the body (hands, feet, etc).		Using a brace to drill a hole is a psycho motor skill.

Skills Training for Tomorrow's Workforce

"under the surface." Skills that could be labeled as "under the surface" include constructive criticism, interpersonal communication, working within constraints, initiating change, and being self-directed.

The process by which skills are acquired is called *skill formation*. Professor Ford has repeatedly emphasized that skill formation cannot be conceptualized in a simple way or equated directly with any particular approach to training and learning. More generally, according to Ford, skill formation can be described as follows:

- A holistic concept that includes the ideas of education, formal vocational training, personal development, on-the-job learning, and experiential learning;
- A dynamic concept that recognizes that skills are culturally related to changing and diverse concepts of technology and work organization; and
- A process-oriented concept that recognizes that skills need to be developed continually over a lifetime.

The recognition that many employees are underskilled is creating a pressing need for more attention to effective skill-formation policies and programs in organizations.

It is striking that only a decade or so ago, concern about technological change centered on the belief that it would lead to a massive process of de-skilling. There are, of course, many industries and job areas in which there has been de-skilling. For example, in industries in which technology is relatively unchanging, such as the automotive industry, some companies have been able to profit by making job roles narrower or by replacing employees with robots or computers. But these types of conditions are not applicable to a lot of industries, and even relatively stable industries eventually modernize and, as a result, need different skills. There is considerable evidence to suggest that technological change usually leads to a need for employees with a higher level of skills.

The notion of higher level skills can be misunderstood easily. It does not mean that employees need more theoretical or academic skills or that employees need to be provided with skills in order to be promoted. What it does mean for employees at all levels is that there is an increased need for a wide range of skills that are more dependent on thinking than on routine, hands-on activity. The next section describes the main types of skills that are currently in short supply.

Skills in Short Supply

Research[6] suggests that the types of skills that are most sought after by industry fall into the following ten areas:

- Self-management
- Conceptual skills
- Creative problem solving
- Holistic thinking
- Self-directed learning skills
- Literacy skills
- Teamwork and group learning
- Communication skills
- Fault diagnosis and rectification

Each of these areas is discussed briefly in the following sections.

Self-Management

The supervisor's role in many organizations has changed significantly in recent years. Instead of taking a dominant role in managing the work and taking responsibility for solving most of the problems, supervisors are tending to adopt a more facilitative role. This change has broadened the employee's role. Employees now have more responsibilities, such as day-to-day operations, quality control, and product output.

Conceptual Skills

In high-technology industries, manual tasks have been replaced with more challenging tasks, and mastering challenging tasks demands familiarity with a new, abstract conceptual language. Examples are as follows:

- In flexible manufacturing systems, the traditional way of working, which is dependent on touch and other senses, is replaced with a pattern of responses to a mental picture of the process, material flow, and its control.

- In banks, handling a cash withdrawal at a teller station via an on-line terminal involves multiple steps and decision points. Tellers need the skills to assess the situation correctly and to make the right choices at each point.

Employees need to understand the concepts that underpin workplace technologies. A sound, conceptual understanding provides a basis for employees to keep up-to-date, even if the technology changes.

Creative Problem Solving

Many employees are finding it necessary to think in new ways to solve complex problems resulting from new technologies or to devise new ways to use technology more effectively. Employees need to be able to apply technological concepts creatively to find new solutions to problems.

Holistic Thinking

The trend in many modern manufacturing and service industries is toward integrated computer systems with as few interfaces as possible. In both the development and manufacture of products, whether they are goods or services, there is a need for thinking that is similarly holistic.

Self-Directed Learning Skills

Employees in many industries have had to contend with rapid changes to products and technologies. To keep abreast of these changes, employees need to be adaptable and to know how to learn quickly and effectively. They also need to be able to seek out new solutions to problems actively and to find new applications of existing technology. This requires such personal characteristics as curiosity, the ability to tolerate uncertainty and ambiguity, and a willingness to innovate and try out hunches.

Literacy Skills

The skilling of employees is partly reliant on their ability to read and write. The development of literacy skills is a prerequisite of the more general process of skill formation.

Information Management

Electronic communication systems and databases have the potential to handle large amounts of information. For example, in the finance industry, a large proportion of employees have direct access via terminal to a range of data-entry, system-control, and maintenance functions. The employees need sophisticated information-management skills in order to distinguish information quality from quantity and to manage these technologies efficiently.

Teamwork and Group Learning

Integrated technologies require high levels of cooperation among employees. Seldom is only one employee involved with each machine; instead, a work group is usually responsible for interacting with a whole technical system. Technologies such as these demand that employees have effective interpersonal skills and that they cooperate in order to achieve group and organizational goals, particularly during system disturbances and breakdowns.

Communication Skills

The ability to get along with other employees and customers has always been important, but today's business practices have increased the importance of communication skills. Not only are oral and written skills important, but knowledge of the languages and cultures of other countries is also becoming important.

Fault Diagnosis and Rectification

In complex technical systems, malfunctions or input errors can have serious and expensive consequences. Employees need to be able to diagnose and rectify problems quickly, even when problems have occurred because of the interaction of different types of technologies, such as electronic, hydraulic, pneumatic, optical, or mechanical.

Successful fault diagnosis and rectification depend on the collection and interpretation of information from a variety of sources and systems. In some jobs, they rely more on hunches and intuition than on routine checking of procedures. Successful fault diagnosis and rectification are dependent on the employees' having internalized an appropriate mental model of the technical system and their ability to do the following:

- To use the mental model to form hunches and test them;
- To discriminate between essential and peripheral considerations;
- To reach adequate solutions based on partial information; and
- To integrate conceptual understandings (diagnosis) with practical hands-on actions (rectification).

The Social Context of Skills

Examination of the main factors that influence skill formation would not be complete without discussing the broader social context of skill. The importance of social factors in skill formation is revealed clearly when one compares between the following:

- Women and men
- New nontrade occupations and traditional trades
- Wage and salary employees
- Immigrant employees and native employees

The skill-formation issues raised in each of these comparisons are examined briefly in this section.[7]

I think she needs <u>down</u>skilling!

Women and Men

The partial segregation of women into jobs that are often of low status and that demand low levels of skill has implications for skill-formation policies and practices. Following are some examples:

- Some occupations often require employees to learn a narrow range of skills, such as word processing or assembly work, and then apply these skills to repetitive tasks under intense time pressure;

- There is often more scope for ongoing skill development in male-dominated occupations than there is in female-dominated occupations, such as healthcare, childcare, library work, and clerical jobs;

- Terms like *semiskilled* and *unskilled* are applied more to female occupations than male occupations;

- Men's and women's vocational skills are at times differently rewarded by employers; and

- In some occupations dominated by females, employees are often expected to pay for their own skill development.

Traditional Trade Classifications

Jobs that have become much more complex as a result of technological change, such as process control, are not recognized as trades. The converse is also true: Some colleges continue to offer courses that they have classified as trade despite the fact that occupational categories have changed.

Wage Versus Salaried Employees

Many organizations traditionally have distinguished between wage and salaried employees. This distinction has carried on Taylor's idea of separating "brain work" from physical work. Wage employees, including many operators and tradespeople, often have not been rewarded for the skills they have learned on the job. However, salaried employees have been rewarded in this way. In addition, wage employees rarely have had the same opportunities for skill development as salaried employees.

Immigrant Employees and Native Employees

Traditionally, the use of immigrant employees has been a way of alleviating skill shortages. It is expected that large numbers of both skilled and unskilled immigrants will increase substantially during the next few decades, and an increasing proportion of the immigrant employees will speak languages other than the native one.

Immigration poses a number of problems in the area of skill training for people engaged in vocational education. These people will need to handle the following problems:

- Differences in opportunities for pay increases in line with skill development for immigrant employees who do not speak the native language;

- The underutilization of immigrant employees' skills because of failure to recognize qualifications or because of language differences;

- The problems of using self-paced training modules with immigrant employees who speak different languages; and

- The difficulty of providing computer literacy and keyboard training to employees who speak different languages.

End Notes

1. See Berg (1985).

2. Adapted from a diagram by G. W. Ford (1988).

3. Adapted from a suggestion by Richard Sweet.

4. Adapted from R. Walton (1985).

5. Adapted from a diagram in Schonberger (1986).

6. For example, see Adler (1986), Bertrand and Noyelle (1988), Curtain (1987), Ford (1984b), and Schonberger (1986).

7. See Pocock (1988).

Bibliography

Adler, P. (1986). New technologies, new skills. *California Management Review, 29*(1).

Bengtsson, L., & Berggren, C. (1986). Workers' future role in the computerized engineering industry. In H. Bullinger (Ed.), *Human factors in manufacturing*. (4th IAO Conference Proceedings, Stuttgart, 1985.) Bedford, UK: IFS Publications.

Berg, P. (1985, May). Technoculture: The symbolic framing of technology in a Volvo plant. *Scandinavian Journal of Management Studies*.

Bertrand, O., & Noyelle, T. (1988). *Human resources in corporate strategy: Technological change in banks and insurance companies in five OECD countries*. Paris: OECD.

Curtain, R. (1987). Work practices agreement in heavy engineering: Potential and limitations. *Work and People, 12*(3).

Davis, E., & Lansbury, R. (Eds.). (1986). *Democracy and control in the workplace*. Melbourne: Longman House.

Eliasson, G., & Ryan, P. (1987). *The human factor in economic and technological change*. Paris: OECD.

Ford, G. (1980). Industrial democracy: Some neglected issues. In R. Lansbury (Ed.), *Democracy in the workplace*. Melbourne: Longman Cheshire.

Ford, G. (1984a). Australia at risk: An underskilled and vulnerable society. In J. Eastwood, J. Reeves, and J. Ryan (Eds.), *Labour essays*. Melbourne: Drummond.

Ford, G. (1984b). Japan as a learning society. *Work and People, 9*(1).

Ford, G. (1988). The dynamics of learning. In J. Hattie, R. Kefford, & P. Porter (Eds.), *Skills technology and management in education*. Deakin, Australia: Australian College of Education.

Ford, G., & Tilley, L. (Eds.). (1986). *Diversity, change and tradition: The environment for industrial democracy in Australia*. Canberra, Australia: AGPS.

Hurschhorn, L. (1984). *Beyond mechanization*. Cambridge, MA: MIT Press.

Kelly, J. (1982). *Scientific management, jobs redesign and work performance*. London: Academic Press.

Koike, K. (1984). Skill formation systems in the US and Japan: A comparative study. In M. Aoki (Ed.), *The economic analysis of the Japanese firm*. Amsterdam: Elsevier Science.

Pocock, B. (1988). *Demanding skill*. North Sydney: Unwin.

Schonberger, R. (1986). *World class manufacturing: The lessons of simplicity applied*. New York: The Free Press.

Taylor, F. (1947). *Principles of scientific management*. New York: Harper & Bros.

Walton, R. (1985, March/April). From control to commitment in the workplace. *Harvard Business Review*.

It is important that an individual's skills match the job

The Terminology of Skill Formation

Terms like *skill, competency,* and *job* are defined differently by different people, and this has led to a lot of confusion. The term *skill* is particularly problematic. If a number of trainers were asked to write down the meaning of the term *skill,* many would probably come up with definitions such as the following:

- The ability to produce something;
- Work that involves hands-on activities; and
- Something you need, along with knowledge, to perform a job.

If the definition of *skill* were restricted to the three meanings given, then the challenge of increasing the skill levels of the work force would be fairly straightforward. Clearly, skills must be more than just physical, hands-on activities.

A model explained in this chapter likens an individual's skills to an iceberg. Many of the skills that contribute to job competence are hidden away "under the surface," just as the bulk of an iceberg is submerged. Training programs that are intended to develop employees' skills need to give appropriate emphasis to under-the-surface skills and to skills that are associated with routine tasks.

In addition to describing skills and the skills-iceberg model, this chapter defines the following terms:

- Job
- Competency
- Competency area
- Task
- Up-skilling
- Cross-skilling
- Multiskilling
- Skill formation
- Broadbanding

In some cases, the definitions given are not the only correct ones. For example, the term *job* has several widely accepted meanings. What has been attempted in this chapter is the development of a set of definitions that are meaningful and that fit together well. These definitions provide a foundation for the rest of this book.

Jobs and Skills

Work in an industry can be thought of as the combination of a job, which is something associated with an organization or an industry, and skills, which are attributes associated with an individual. These two components are illustrated in Figure 2.1.

Firgure 2.1. Jobs and Skilled Employees—The Two Halves of Work Activities

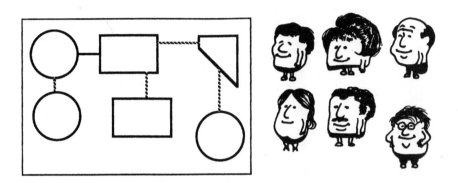

In this chapter, each of the two components, jobs and skilled employees, is examined separately, and then the relationship between the two is examined.

Terms Associated with Jobs

This section defines the main terms that are of interest to trainers in describing the work activities within an organization. These terms are as follows:

- Job
- Competency area
- Competency
- Task

The relationship between these four terms is shown in Figure 2.2. It might be helpful to try to relate each definition to this composite picture as you read further.

Figure 2.2. The Terms Associated with Jobs

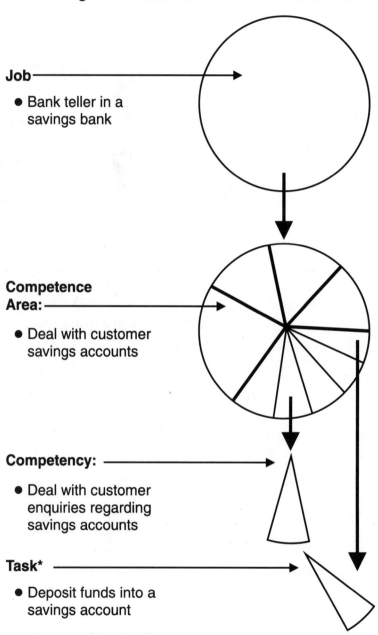

Job
- Bank teller in a savings bank

Competence Area:
- Deal with customer savings accounts

Competency:
- Deal with customer enquiries regarding savings accounts

Task*
- Deposit funds into a savings account

*****Note.** As explained in the text, this is also a competency.

Job

The term *job* can be used in different ways:

- "This job will only take an hour."
- "I just got a new job."
- "Let's go out on the job."

In this book, the term has a specific meaning: A job consists of the work performed by an individual. For example, bank teller in a savings bank is a job.

Competency Area

Jobs can be broken down into competency areas. Another word for competency area is *duty*. A competency area is a cluster of interrelated competencies. For example, handling customer savings accounts is a competency area. Competencies may be grouped into areas in a variety of ways; refer to Chapter 5 for details.

Competency

Competencies may be pictured as the building blocks of jobs. A competency is a task, process, or strategy that is part of what an individual employee does in his or her job. For example, the competencies of a bank teller might include the following:

- Deposit funds into a savings account; and
- Answer customer enquiries regarding savings accounts.

Performance criteria are usually established for each competency. These indicate minimum standards for satisfactory performance and are used to determine whether an employee can perform a job adequately.

Task

The term *task* refers to a particular sort of competency. All tasks are competencies, but not all competencies are tasks. A task is a competency if it meets the following criteria:

- Is routine and predictable;
- Involves a sequence of steps;
- Has a definite start and finish; and
- Produces a tangible outcome.

The relationship between tasks and competencies can be better understood by considering the two examples of competencies given earlier. The first, deposit funds into a savings account, is a routine procedure. It results in a specific outcome, a different account total. This competency is a task.

The second competency, answer customer inquiries regarding savings accounts, is not as straightforward. There are many sorts of customer inquiries that a teller has to answer. Although most banks have procedural guidelines for answering inquiries, a teller may have to handle situations that are not specified in the guidelines. To handle customer inquiries adequately, the teller needs to draw on his or her interpersonal skills, initiative, and knowledge of bank procedures, services, and systems. A competency like this is not classified as a task.

The Nature of Skill

The term *skill* can refer to any of the abilities that an employee has, such as the following:

- Applying knowledge to the job;
- Expressing oneself clearly;

- Performing calculations;
- Aligning two surfaces;
- Relating to others;
- Remembering facts;
- Judging volumes;
- Working quickly and accurately;
- Acting on hunches;
- Leading groups; and
- Learning and adapting.

The discussion in the last section of terms that are associated with jobs left employees and their skills out of the picture. But trying to discuss jobs without taking skills into account is a little like trying to use a two-dimensional drawing to represent a three-dimensional object. In Figure 2.2, a two-dimensional triangular symbol was used to represent competencies and tasks. What gives the shape volume, a third dimension, is the mixture of skills that each employee brings to the job.

Types of Skills

Task Skills

As a first step to understanding the skill dimension, consider the skills that an employee uses to deposit funds into a savings account. These sorts of skills will be called *task skills*. Task skills are represented as a three-dimensional cone in Figure 2.3. The cone is the three-dimensional equivalent of the shape that was used to represent a task in Figure 2.2.

Figure 2.3 shows the task-skills cone floating in a murky fluid. This fluid, which appears impenetrable the deeper the

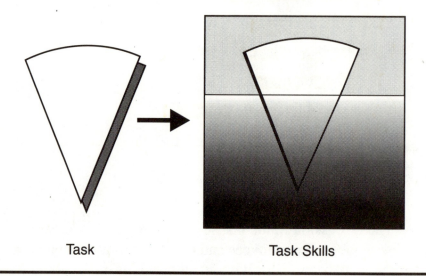

Figure 2.3. Task and Task Skills

cone goes, is intended to represent the internal processes that accompany task performance. Tasks themselves will vary and some are more straightforward than others. Regardless of such differences, when a task is first being learned, each step poses a problem. The employee may believe that there is not enough information to know what to do next, and he or she may often feel uninformed.[1]

As time goes on, the employee gains more experience, and the procedure seems easier to follow. More and more of the task becomes routine, and the skills that are used are, in terms of our model, "above the surface." This means that the employee can think about, talk about, and demonstrate the skills.

The change in task skills that occurs as an employee goes from beginner to accomplished is shown in Figure 2.4. With experience, the employee uses more skills that are above the surface.

Most of what researchers know about skills and tasks is derived from studies of experienced employees. This is because

Figure 2.4. The Effect of Experience on Task Skills

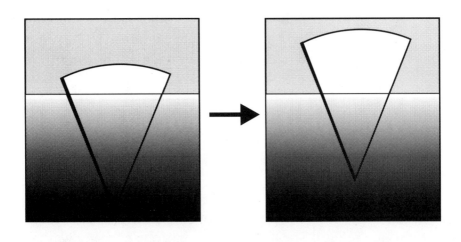

as tasks are mastered, more of the procedure becomes above the surface and, hence, visible to researchers. However, the same task may be experienced quite differently by an inexperienced employee, and this fact needs to be considered if reference notes will be designed or if training will be provided.

So far, the discussion has been restricted to the skills needed to perform a task. If the model is expanded to include different competencies, not just tasks, it will include areas that are not well understood. That is, in terms of the skills-iceberg model, we are beginning to think about the under-the-surface aspects of skill. It is very important that trainers take these under-the-surface skills into account. The fact that such skills are hard to discuss and analyze is no reason to neglect them in training.

The skills that an employee uses to perform a particular job or to learn a new competency area resemble an iceberg (Figure 2.5). Task skills are at the core of the iceberg and are mainly above the surface. Surrounding this core, and mainly under the surface, are a variety of other types of skills. Despite the fact that they are not very highly visible to vocational-education researchers, they contribute enormously to workplace competence.

To simplify the discussion, these other skills have been grouped into four clusters, and these are examined in the rest of this section.[2] The four clusters of skills are the following:

- Task-management skills
- Work-environment skills
- Workplace-learning skills
- Interpersonal skills

Remember that the skills-iceberg model is only one way of simplifying reality. The model represents one of many ways of grouping skill types. It does not represent the only way of grouping skill types, nor does it imply that there *are* rigid boundaries between the different skill types. This model should not be construed to be representative of the complexity of employee skills, and the reality is far more subtle than this model implies.

Task-Management Skills

Following are examples of task-management skills:

- Plan an activity to minimize waste.
- Perform a number of tasks in the appropriate order.
- Manage system failure.
- Apply standards.
- Anticipate and avoid problems.

In order to perform most jobs competently, employees need to coordinate a range of tasks. Task skills and task-management

Figure 2.5. The Skills-Iceberg Model of an Individual's Skills

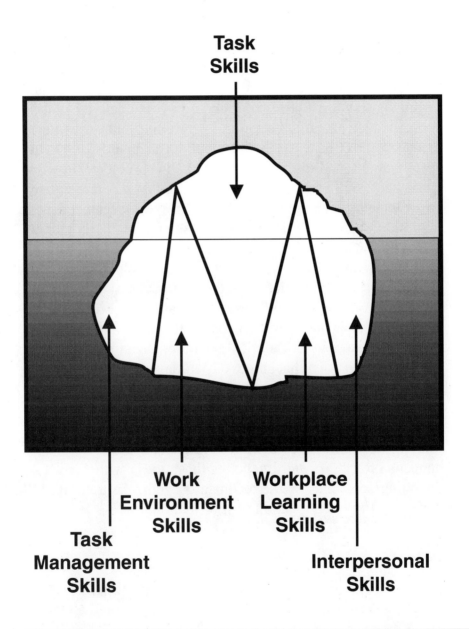

The Terminology of Skill Formation

skills are not the same. An employee may be able to perform a task, but without the ability to coordinate a number of tasks and competencies to achieve the most effective outcome, the employee could not be considered fully competent.

In trade areas such as plumbing or carpentry, the task-management skills might include timing a piece of work so that it is finished on schedule, using raw materials with minimum waste, completing each part of a sequence in the right order, and beginning the task by thinking about how the activity will be completed. In manufacturing and processing industries, task-management skills could include applying standards, achieving specifications, and anticipating and avoiding problems. In office work, such skills might include ensuring that data are entered correctly into a computer, that files are kept organized with minimum waste, and that precautions such as regularly making backup disks are taken.

Task-management skills rely in part on close integration between one's mental picture of the technical system and practical hands-on experience. These two areas often get out of sync. It is almost as if there are two compartments in the brain: one that stores abstractions, theories, and rationalizations about how one acts, and another that guides day-to-day work activities. The concepts stored in this second compartment may not always be correct. Misinformation and distorted concepts may be stored from schooldays, or even earlier, and never be corrected. Unless training brings out the employees' personal ideas about what happens on the job and integrates these ideas with the actual operating principles of the technical system, the training will have only limited impact on skill formation.

Work-Environment Skills

Following are examples of work-environment skills:

- ♦ Work effectively within constraints.

- Work effectively in a particular organization.
- Change unhealthy, unsafe aspects of work.

The extent to which an individual employee has the ability to cope with the peculiarities of each job environment greatly influences his or her competence. Jobs and work sites vary considerably with regard to elements such as the following:

- Location (heights, confined spaces);
- Physical demands (heavy equipment, lifting, standing);
- Manual dexterity (using a keyboard, fine manual control);
- Atmospheric conditions (dust, irritants, noise, smells);
- Outputs (discrete objects, services, continuous production); and
- Time pressures (technology-paced, customer pressures).

In any particular workplace or job, some employees cope more adequately than others. Employees who do adjust quickly may be said to understand the job or the technology. More correctly, adjusting suggests a combination of the following two factors:

- Having skills that match the demands of the job; and
- Having the necessary skills to press for changes to unsafe, unhealthy aspects of the work environment.

Both factors can be categorized as work-environment skills.

Workplace-Learning Skills

Following are examples of workplace-learning skills:

- Be self-directed in learning.
- Be adaptable to change.
- Initiate change.
- Train others.
- Encourage workplace learning.

Some employees are thoughtful and quick to build on their experiences, whereas others seem to make the same mistakes repeatedly. Although the factors that contribute to mindfulness are not well understood, it is clear that the abilities to reflect, learn, and support the learning of others are central to workplace competence. Research suggests that employees who have effective learning skills have the following abilities:

- They can think about and discuss their own learning needs.
- They can overcome the disadvantages of their limited formal education.
- They are confident about keeping up, despite rapid change.
- They are good at investigating situations, presenting complex information logically, and drawing general conclusions from particular observations.

At the present time, when there is a rapid upgrading of new technology, workplace-learning skills are particularly important. Even if trainers could keep abreast of these changes—and in many instances they cannot—time constraints would make it impossible to cover all the specific types of systems and equipment in formal training programs. Employees need skills in learning on the job, so that they can build on their conceptual understanding and use it to operate new technologies with flexibility and innovativeness. An important aspect of workplace-learning skills is the ability to transfer what is learned in one situation to others or, when appropriate, to recognize differences in systems and to modify the mental picture of the work process accordingly.

Interpersonal Skills

Following are examples of interpersonal skills:

- Maintain good work relations.
- Work in a team.
- Discuss workplace issues and problems.

Interpersonal skills are more commonly associated with jobs such as customer service or administrative work than with more technical jobs, but this is a mistake. The skills needed to relate well to others and to work as part of a team are important in almost all jobs. For example, people who work long shifts have to spend many hours together, and someone who annoys everyone else can hinder work enormously.

People like air-traffic controllers and process operators have to coordinate their work with others. Good interpersonal skills are essential in these sorts of jobs. The introduction of more participative work practices, such as work teams and safety committees, also means that effective interpersonal skills are more important than ever before.

Interpersonal skills are also needed so that work issues and problems can be discussed in a group. For example, in jobs such as nursing and teaching, stressful situations arise that need to be talked through with others as part of day-to-day work. The workplace reforms that are currently being introduced in Australia are also resulting in a lot of issues that need to be discussed and negotiated in a group.

The Relationship Between Jobs and Employees' Skills

Having considered terms used to describe jobs and skills separately, we can now look at terms used to describe the relationship between the two. Each employee has his or her own mixture of skills, only some of which are used in a particular job. There is never an exact fit between a job and an individual's skills.

A number of terms are used to describe the process of skill development and the links between jobs and skills:

- Up-skilling
- Cross-skilling
- Multiskilling
- Skill formation

These terms are defined in this section.

Up-Skilling

Up-skilling refers to the process by which employees acquire additional skills at higher levels of complexity (Figure 2.6). The complexity of a work activity is related to the extent to which under-the-surface skills and mental processes are involved. Up-skilling is not about encouraging employees to become theoreticians or academics, but it is related to mastery of more complex competencies.

Cross-Skilling

Cross-skilling refers to helping employees to develop more diverse skills (Figure 2.6). It is often accompanied by a reduction in demarcation barriers between jobs or trades.

Multiskilling

Multiskilling refers to a way of organizing work so that employees are able to perform a wider range of competencies. For example, in addition to operating a machine, employees might also be expected to do preventive-maintenance work. Multiskilling necessitates a general increase in skills, both vertically, in terms of complexity, and horizontally, in terms of diversity (Figure 2.6). Its introduction needs to be accompanied by a reduction in demarcation barriers, so that employees are better

Figure 2.6. Up-Skilling, Multiskilling, and Cross-Skilling

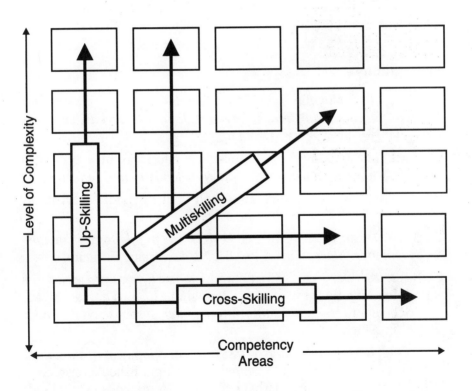

The Terminology of Skill Formation

able to complete whole tasks without having to hand over their work to others.

Skill Formation

Skill formation refers to the general process of skill development and recognizes the links between skills and other aspects of organizational technoculture. (Skill formation is discussed more fully in Chapter 1.)

End Notes

1. See Card, Moran, and Newell (1983), and Carrol and Mack (1985).

2. The skills-iceberg model draws on Orna (1971), Card, Moran, and Newell (1983), and Mansfield and Shelborn (1988).

Bibliography

Bertrand, O., & Noyelle, T. (1986). *Changing technology, skills and skill formation in French, German, Japanese, Swedish and US financial firms.* Paris: OECD.

Birch, T. (1986, May 5). Man-machine interfaces in a computer controlled pharmaceutical factory. *Chemistry and Industry.*

Briggs, R. (1988, February). How will your operators react in an emergency? *Process Engineering.*

Card, S., Moran, T., & Newell, A. (1983). *The psychology of human-computer interaction.* Hillsdale, NJ: Lawrence Erlbaum.

Carrol, J., & Mack, R. (1985). Learning to use a word processor: By doing, by thinking and by knowing. In J. Thomas & M. Schneider, *Human factors in computer systems.* Northwood, N.J.: Alben Publishing.

Mansfield, B., & Shelborn, B. (1988). *The development of standards in generic aspects of competence.* Unpublished consultants report produced by Barbara Shelborn Associates, Wakefield, UK.

Marsick, V. (1987). *Learning in the workplace*. Beckenham, UK: Croom Helm.

Orna, E. (1971). *The analysis and training of certain engineering craft occupations* (Report No. 2). London: Engineering Industry Training Board.

Wilkinson, B. (1982, December 9). Battling it [sic] out on the factory floor. *New Scientist*.

Trainers face a number of gaps in what is understood about training to meet industry needs

Challenges For Trainers

In recent years, a broad vision of the directions that need to be taken in order to reform manufacturing and service industries has been created. Trainers are expected to play a central role in the implementation of this broad vision, but the difficulties of doing so should not be underestimated.

Even the terms associated with skill formation are used inconsistently, which can be confusing for trainers. To add to the difficulties, there has been only a limited amount of research done into the sorts of skills and training strategies that are most appropriate for modern workplace equipment, systems, and processes. As a result, there are many gaps in what is known about the training strategies that best suit modern industries.

Seven Challenges for Trainers

As attempts are made to implement the broad vision of industry revitalization, trainers are likely to have to grapple with a range of difficult issues. In this chapter, seven issues that are likely to be particularly problematic are discussed:

- Recognizing and supporting on-the-job learning;
- Providing training in under-the-surface skills;

* Grounding training in organizational technoculture;
* Recognizing the active nature of learning;
* Supporting internal-labor market strategies;
* Ensuring equal access to training; and
* Introducing integrated training solutions.

Recognizing and Supporting On-the-Job Learning

Employees who are already employed in industry will be offered more training in the future. One of the best ways to acquire new skills is to learn them on the job alongside more experienced employees. On-the-job training and learning are particularly important because industry tends to import workplace

Trainers Will Need to Emphasize Under-the-Surface Skills When Training.

technology and use it well before educational institutions have incorporated it into vocational programs. Time lags such as this have occurred in a number of job areas, including photo-typesetting and desktop publishing, computer-aided design (CAD), computer-aided manufacture (CAM), NC machining, and word processing. When there is a delay in introducing new technology into formal training programs, on-the-job training may be the only training option that is available initially.

On-the-job training raises a number of challenges for trainers and others who are involved in planning vocational education. Here are some examples:

- Mechanisms need to be established so that skills that are learned on the job are recognized and are formally accredited.

- On-the-job training needs to be planned in such a way that it complements other types of training provided in-house or by other providers.

- Employees and managers need to agree on matters such as the relationship between on-the-job and off-the-job training and the way in-house work assessments are to be done.

- An effective on-the-job trainer needs to have skills in instructional planning, explaining, demonstrating, and supervising. Training in areas such as these will be needed by employees who are required to train others on the job.

Providing Training in Under-the-Surface Skills

Chapter 2 distinguishes between task skills and under-the-surface skills. Task skills are associated with activities that meet the criteria on the following page.

- They are routine and predictable.
- They involve a sequence of steps.
- They have a definite start and finish.
- They produce a tangible outcome.

Training that deals only with task skills is usually fairly straightforward. In contrast, under-the-surface skills can be much more difficult to deal with adequately in training. As stated in Chapter 2, under-the-surface skills can be grouped into the following four areas:

- Task-management skills, such as using a mental picture of a process to anticipate and thereby avoid problems;
- Work-environment skills, such as changing unhealthy, unsafe aspects of work;
- Workplace-learning skills, such as using new technology in innovative ways; and
- Work-relationship skills, such as working effectively as a team member.

In order to perform many competencies, employees will need to use a mixture of task skills and under-the-surface skills. Traditional approaches to training have often overemphasized task skills and either treated under-the-surface skills indirectly or even ignored them altogether. This is unfortunate. Task skills are often associated with particular technologies or processes, whereas many of the skills presently in short supply—such as the abilities to adapt to change, to generalize from specific occurrences, to work cooperatively with others, to apply knowledge in innovative ways, to distinguish between different types of phenomena, to solve problems, to manage complex processes, to learn on the job—are located under the surface.

It is important that training covers both task skills and under-the-surface skills adequately. This means that more effort will have to be devoted to developing training approaches that foster task-management skills, work-environment skills, workplace-learning skills, and work-relationship skills.

Grounding Training in Organizational Technoculture

As discussed in Chapter 1, the term *technoculture* refers to the complex pattern of relations between technology and the social system in an organization.

The main aspects of technoculture are related to the following four areas:

- Industrial relations
- The nature of technology
- Work organization
- Skill formation

To be successful, approaches to skills training within an organization need to be grounded in these four technocultural dimensions. Somehow, trainers will have to find ways to develop and maintain links between training and organizational technoculture. There is no standard way of achieving this. It requires thinking about questions such as the following:

Industrial relations. What aspects of industrial disputes are related to training or the lack of it? What training approaches are needed to make employee relations function more effectively within the organization?

Work groups. What are the implications of the structure of work groups for training content and delivery? What training is needed to make work groups function and relate to one another more adequately? How can training contribute to the delegation of more responsibility and accountability to each work group?

Technology. How does/could the organization's technology support learning and job performance? What implications does the nature of the technology have for training? What training is needed to facilitate the choice and introduction of the right kind of technology into the workplace? What assumptions and values are inherent in an organization's technology, and what effect do these have on training?

Skills. What skills do employees need? How do work groups use each member's skills? How are the necessary skills best learned and maintained? How adequate are present training approaches for developing different types of skills?

Recognizing the Active Nature of Learning

Research into learning has revealed that learners are active when they are trying to master a new competency area. Each new competency represents unfamiliar territory for the learner. Somehow, using previous experience and documentary information such as user manuals and system cues, the learner has to try to find a way through that new territory (Figure 3.1).

It is like trying to navigate through an unfamiliar waterway. At first, the journey is full of problems that must be solved with insufficient knowledge. Numerous decisions have to be made at every stage. It is easy to get lost and then to have to retrace one's steps. The waterway illustrated in Figure 3.1(a) is simple compared with the challenges that learners face when trying to master the competencies needed in high-technology industries.

Gradually, though, the journey becomes more and more routine. With greater familiarity, the learner makes fewer mistakes and the associated dangers are minimized. Little by little, a competency that at first seemed to be composed of multiple

Figure 3.1. Learning a New Competency Is Like Trying to Navigate Through an Unfamiliar Waterway [4]

(a) Navigation as problem solving:

Beginner's view of the waterway showing route taken

(b) Navigation as a routine process:

Experienced person's view of the waterway showing route taken

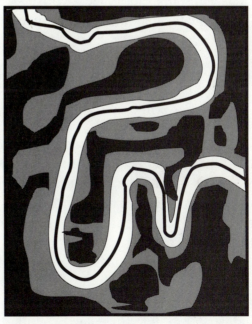

Challenges for Trainers

problems begins to seem more straightforward and to consist of more routine pathways (Figure 3.1b).

The metaphor of learners as navigators helps one to visualize the way in which adults learn. Instead of thinking of training programs as ways of transferring skills and workplace knowledge into passive learners, trainers need to recognize that learning is an active process. Training programs should be structured so that they encourage learners to help one another, to understand and learn from the technical system's own prompts and help mechanisms, and to take responsibility for their own learning.

Supporting Internal-Labor-Market Strategies

There are two broad strategies by which organizations can meet their skill requirements:[1]

- An external-labor-market strategy, which involves dismissing employees whose skills are obsolete or inadequate and hiring employees who have skills that are needed; or

- An internal-labor-market strategy, which emphasizes skill development by continual training coupled with long-term employment security.

During the 1980s, many organizations were reluctant to train their staffs because of high worker mobility and the possible loss of employees to other organizations. Recent business downturns forced many companies to cease hiring apprentices, and this development increased their reliance on external labor to fill skills shortages.

As the experience of many industries confirms, hiring employees away from other organizations is an ineffective approach in the long run. In industries such as the airline industry, present shortages of skilled workers can be directly attributed to cutbacks in opportunities for skill formation and an overreliance on the external-labor market.

One of the most significant changes occurring at present is that many organizations are shifting from external- to internal-labor-market strategies; they are attempting to develop the skills of their employees rather than recruiting skilled workers who have been trained elsewhere. For this reason, trainers are likely to become more involved in the long-term skill development of existing employees. This will influence the trainers' instructional approaches, program structures, and delivery modes.

Ensuring Equal Access to Training

Much of the present discussion about changes in skills training appears to assume that the work force is homogeneous. In fact, today's work force is very diverse, and those responsible for training will have to work hard to ensure that each employee is appropriately trained.

Some of the groups of employees who are in danger of being overlooked in present discussions about the restructuring of jobs and industry are as follows:

- Freelance workers in industries such as the clothing industry;
- Employees who work part-time and are not members of a union;
- Employees who speak different languages;
- Employees who have low levels of literacy and math skills;
- Employees who do not want to be retrained; and
- Employees who have left work because of family needs and want to return to their old jobs.

The trend toward internal-labor-market strategies could itself contribute to inequality in training. Training programs designed to enhance employees' skills are being offered in many large organizations, but those who are unemployed or who work for small companies could easily miss out. To keep this from happening, governmental agencies may need to intervene.

Introducing Integrated Training Solutions

Just as there is a trend toward workplace technologies that involve fewer barriers between departments so training programs for these technologies also need to include occupational areas that were previously distinct. The blurring of boundaries between areas like mechanics and electronics and the gradual reduction of demarcation barriers between jobs will need to be accompanied by well-integrated skills training. This does not mean that specialist skills-formation programs need to be very general, but that there is an increasing demand for generalists who are familiar with a range of systems and their interconnections. A challenge for trainers will be to develop training that reflects these cross-disciplinary connections.

End Note

1. Sweet (1988).

Bibliography

Buchanan, D., & Bessant, J. (1985). Failure, uncertainty and control: The role of operators in a computer integrated production system. *Journal of Management Studies, 22*(3).

Hayes, C., Anderson, A., & Fonda, N. (1984). *Competence and competition: Training and education in the Federal Republic of Germany, the United States and Japan.* London: National Economic Development Office.

Singer, R. (1978). Motor skills and learning strategies. In H. O'Neil (Ed.), *Learning strategies*. New York: Academic Press.

Sweet, R. (1988). Industry restructuring and workforce reskilling. *Work and People, 13*(1 & 2).

Tayler, D. (1987). Advanced manufacturing technology: The implication for human resource strategies. *Applied Ergonomics, 19*(1).

US Manufacturing Studies Board. (1986). *Human resource practices for implementing advanced manufacturing technology*. Washington, DC: National Academy Press.

Research needs to be conducted to collect information about skills and training needs

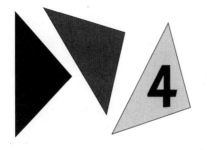

Investigate Skills and Training Issues

Trainers often have to collect information about skills and training needs and use it to design training materials and programs. Although they might not use the term *research* to describe these activities, that is exactly what these activities are. Such research may not be very formal and it may not consist of an orderly sequence of steps, but it is still a systematic attempt to collect information to solve workplace problems and to overcome skill deficiencies. This approach to research is called *action research.*

It would be unrealistic, however, to suggest that trainers should be equipped to investigate every workplace issue that arises. Sometimes problems occur in large organizations and across industries that call for experienced researchers to collect information and report their findings. Such studies often take a lot of time and considerable expertise in areas like data analysis and organizational behavior. Experienced researchers would normally use an approach that is more formal than action research.

This chapter covers both action research and more formal approaches. It describes how a trainer can perform the following:

- Conduct an exploratory study;
- Analyze a task; and
- Prepare a competency guide.

Chapter 4 also briefly discusses more formal types of research, such as labor-market studies and large-scale needs analysis.

Types of Workplace Research

As Figure 4.1 indicates, there are three closely associated approaches used by trainers to perform workplace investigations:

- Exploratory studies of workplace problems;
- Analysis of training needs; and
- Analysis of tasks.

Figure 4.1. The Main Workplace-Research Activities

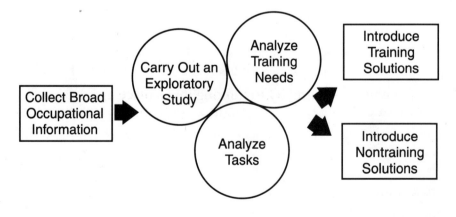

Figure 4.1 also indicates that these three approaches take place against a background of information that exists within most industries and large organizations. This information consists of the following:

- Position statements
- Work-assessment records
- Various statistics
- Procedure manuals

It is important to note that Figure 4.1 does not capture the uncertainty and frustration that often surround attempts to understand workplace problems. Doing workplace research is not a simple, four-step process from which a neat set of training and nontraining solutions emerge, and this is not meant to be implied by the figure. An important personal quality needed in order to study skills and training problems is the ability to tolerate uncertainty as solutions gradually emerge from investigations.

A second point to note is that workplace studies can all too easily focus on tasks that are routine and self-contained. Many of the skills discussed in this book are difficult to identify and describe. Research approaches have not been developed yet that can deal adequately with all the different under-the-surface skills that employees in modern organizations depend on.

Collect Occupational Data

Research related directly to training takes place against a background of more general occupational information. Some of this is available from the human-resource management department or representative and some from formal studies conducted by government departments, employer groups, and large organizations. Such studies include industry analysis, labor-market analysis, and occupational analysis.[1]

The purpose of each of these is as follows:

* Industry analysis examines the boundaries of a particular industry, looks at levels of industry activity, and assesses likely industry growth and employment.
* Labor-market analysis focuses on the present and anticipated numbers of people who can be employed across a range of jobs. It considers who is available as well as present or anticipated demand.
* Occupational analysis is concerned with the present and anticipated jobs in an occupational category and with the competencies that make up each job.

The information gathered from industry, the labor market, and occupational analyses is used for the following activities:

* Training-needs analysis
* Job classification
* Wage setting
* Clarification of duties and responsibilities
* Promotion planning
* Health and safety investigations
* Individual work assessments

If a study of training issues must be conducted, become familiar with the background information that is available and, after checking that it is up-to-date, use it when necessary.

Carry Out an Exploratory Study

Many problems that arise in the workplace could indicate that training is needed. Such problems include the following:

* High turnover

- Low product-quality
- Inadequate customer-service
- Frequent accidents
- Customer complaints
- Industrial disputes
- Delays in agreed deadlines
- Low productivity
- Low morale

Difficulties in any of these areas can be caused by inadequate or inappropriate training, but they may also be caused by factors that are totally unrelated to training. For this reason, the first phase of any workplace study usually is to carry out an exploratory investigation.

The purpose of the exploratory investigation is to examine the issues and to begin to think about the causes of the problems that have surfaced. Thinking broadly about the problems before committing to a particular course of action is likely to save time and money in the long run. There is no need to worry too much about getting a balanced sample of opinions like those resulting from a more formal, large-scale study. Try instead to get a general feeling for what is happening. This might involve talking with a cross section of the people involved, including those who surfaced the problem. If appropriate, collect and examine relevant documents such as production records, minutes of meetings, and letters of complaint. Then talk again with some of the people involved. Reflect on the feelings that are revealed and think about the factors that might be contributing, such as these:

- The way industrial relations have been handled within a particular organization;

- Management style;
- The equipment and software being used and the way they have been introduced;
- The apparent levels of employees' skills;
- The way the work and employees are organized;
- The way rewards, both overt ones like pay increases and more subtle ones such as employee privileges and employee-management relations, operate;
- The staffing levels;
- The availability of adequate training;
- The way changes to systems and procedures have been introduced; and
- The overall health of the organization or of specific departments.

Exploring the problems and thinking about causes will lead to one of the following three conclusions:

The problems are not related to training. In this situation, the issues may be handled by communicating with others who are more directly responsible, so that the problems are solved by the most appropriate department or individual.

The problems may be reduced by training. In this case, additional research may need to be done. This might involve needs analysis, task analysis, or a combination of both.

The problems are directly related to poor training. The term *training* here covers much more than formal classroom training. A training program might include a combination of the following elements:

- On-the-job learning under supervision;

- Job rotation;
- Computer-aided learning;
- Trainer upgrading;
- Provision of job aids;
- Self-directed learning using workbooks;
- Provision of training resources; and
- Training in a simulated work environment.

The preliminary conclusion that problems are being caused by a training deficiency does not necessarily mean that a training program will be offered. Budget limitations, previous commitments, training-staff availability, and similar factors can defer an organization's training plans. But, assuming that training can be provided, the exploratory study might well have revealed all the information needed to set up a training program.

Analyze Training Needs

Needs analysis refers to a study of the difference between the present conditions and the desired conditions. The term *conditions* refers to things like knowledge, behaviors, attitudes, outputs, and error rates. A training need is said to exist when there is a gap between the present conditions and the desired conditions that can be remedied by training.

Needs analysis is an interesting area in training. A great deal has been written about it, and many advertisements for trainers include needs analysis as a key responsibility. Nevertheless, few formal needs studies have actually been conducted by trainers. The main reason for this discrepancy appears to be that a lot of what has been written about the area reflects a very superficial view of workplace life.[2] Reading through this literature, one could easily get the impression that the following statements are true:

It is easy to describe "actual" conditions and "desired" conditions. In fact, there are few jobs for which it is possible to describe in detail either actual employee knowledge, skills, outputs, and so on or desired ones.

The idea of a desired condition is neutral and commonly agreed on. In fact, in most organizations, skilled employees, managers, union officials, and new employees all have different views of desired conditions.

Employees are passive and do not contribute much to organizational life. In reality employees actively contribute to what happens in the workplace. The idea that training needs can be determined by management alone underemphasizes things like employees' pride in their work, the proactive role that employees take to keep systems running, and the fact that different employees have different abilities.

There is no change in technology. In fact, there has been a big increase in the complexity of technology in organizations within recent years. The concepts of needs assessment are not always helpful in dealing with such changes.

This last area, which deals with assessing training needs brought about by new technology, can be particularly troublesome. For example, consider the introduction of word processors. During the phasing-in period, few people knew what skills were needed to operate a word processor competently. Very few word-processing training programs were based on systematic needs assessment. Instead, as with most new technology, training was by trial and error with the help of system manuals.

The main implication of all this is that trainers conducting needs-assessment studies should take the time to understand the factors that contribute to workplace problems. It helps if they understand that needs assessment is a type of applied research in which the trainer cannot stand outside the area being studied and take precise measures of skills deficiencies or training needs in the way that a scientist in a laboratory might.

Although it is outside the scope of this book to describe in detail how to perform this type of research, trainers should have some understanding of the process and be able to work with people who have special skills in this area. These people might be other trainers with particular expertise in needs assessment, consultants, or curriculum experts.

The two broad approaches to performing needs analysis are called *action research* and *descriptive-survey research*. These two approaches differ in terms of the following:

Role of the researcher. In action research, the researcher is usually directly involved with those being studied. In contrast, a researcher doing descriptive-survey research tends to stand outside the issues being studied.

Purpose of the research. Action research is primarily concerned with bringing about change; just the act of studying workplace problems may generate solutions. In descriptive-survey research, the main purpose is to accurately describe problems with a view toward suggesting solutions but not necessarily implementing them.

Vocational educators need to have a good understanding of action research and they should also have some familiarity with the more formal descriptive-survey approach. Each of these is described in the following sections.

Action Research

It is easiest to visualize action research as a series of spirals of activity that come closer and closer to the problem and contribute to its solution along the way (Figure 4.2). Each spiral is made up of four areas of activity: planning, acting, observing, and reflecting. Action research consists of the following:

Figure 4.2. Action-Research Spirals[3]

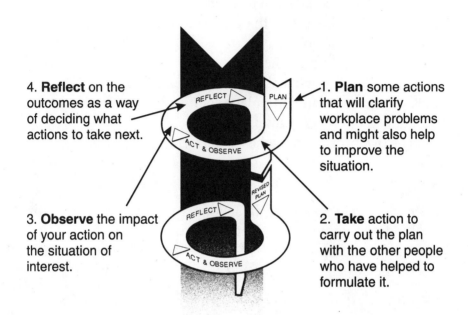

1. **Plan** some actions that will clarify workplace problems and might also help to improve the situation.

2. **Take** action to carry out the plan with the other people who have helped to formulate it.

3. **Observe** the impact of your action on the situation of interest.

4. **Reflect** on the outcomes as a way of deciding what actions to take next.

- Planning actions that will clarify workplace problems and might help to improve the situation;

- Carrying out the plan with the people who helped to formulate it;

- Observing the impact of the plan; and

- Reflecting on the outcomes as a way of deciding what actions to take next.

Action research recognizes that when a trainer tries to investigate workplace problems, two other processes inevitably occur:

- Talking with people and collecting information begins the problem-solving process. Action research recognizes that the investigation itself can contribute to solving problems.

- Partial solutions can be introduced as soon as they emerge. Action research recognizes that solutions can be tried out while problems are still being understood.

In action research, remedies can be evolving while the researcher continues into the second, third, or even fourth spiral of planning, acting, observing, and reflecting.

Seeing needs analysis as a form of action research gives rise to an emphasis on close integration of data and results. In contrast to descriptive-survey research, in which the goal normally would be a final report, an action-research approach lends itself to the ongoing sharing of data with employees and management and the integration of the needs-assessment investigation with areas such as production planning. If this approach is used, both needs assessment and the training function generally are more likely to be seen as relevant.

Descriptive-Survey Research[4]

Descriptive-survey research is more formal than action research. It is typically thought of as consisting of four stages (Figure 4.3). Descriptive-survey research would normally be carried out only in large organizations or across industries and would most commonly involve the help of someone experienced in this sort of research, such as an outside consultant or a curriculum specialist. This approach is like market research, in which employees are viewed as "consumers" and training programs as "products."

The four stages of descriptive-survey research are listed on the following three pages.

Figure 4.3. The Four Stages of Descriptive Survey Research

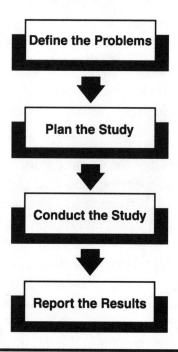

Stage 1: Define the problem to be examined. This stage coincides with exploratory research. It involves exploring different aspects of workplace problems, such as these:

- How much commitment is there to solving the problem?
- What problem is occurring and why?
- Where is the problem occurring?
- When does the problem happen?
- Who is involved in the problematic situation?
- How does the problem occur?

Stage 2: Plan the study. Planning involves deciding on the research objectives and expected outcomes of the study, preparing a formal research proposal, and recruiting assistance for the project. For example, recruiting a consultant and establishing a project team to oversee the study would be done at this stage. At the end of the planning stage, the following should be clarified:

- The type of information that is needed for the study and its availability;
- The approximate cost of performing the study;
- Any extra resources required, such as computing assistance to analyze the data; and
- The degree of accuracy expected.

Stage 3: Conduct the study. Conducting the study typically involves the following:

- Working with consultants and with a project team;
- Reviewing documentary information;
- Deciding who is to be studied (the population) and how a representative cross section of the population's views will be obtained (the sample);
- Developing and using survey methods to collect information; and
- Collecting and analyzing data.

Stage 4: Report the results. The method that will be used to report the findings should be thought out carefully, especially if the findings will be presented to a large organization. Reporting the information does not necessarily mean that a report must be prepared. A number of reports with different focuses and degrees of detail might be prepared for each relevant section and level. For example, one report might be prepared for the chief executive officer, another report for the personnel manager, and another for the training department. Reporting the information might also include other approaches, such as live presentations, in-house newsletters, and videos.

The principal purpose of reporting results is to suggest ways of solving the workplace problems that led to the study. Thought needs to be given to how best to get support for the proposed solutions. The most important things to remember are as follows:

- Make sure that the proposal is clear.
- Back up the proposal with research data.
- Present the findings and proposed solutions to the people who have the authority to approve them.

Workplace Research Methods

Despite the differences between these two approaches, the methods available for data collection are the same (Figure 4.4). There are methodological differences, however, which show up when one looks closely at how these general methods are applied.

For example, consider questionnaires. In action research, the questionnaire would probably be used to explore issues. It might be developed collaboratively by the researcher and a group of employees and managers. The collected data would be discussed widely in the organization, so that emerging solutions would reflect a fair compromise between the differing viewpoints. An essential ingredient of action research is an openness to finding out what is the real problem and a commitment to introducing workable solutions.

In descriptive-survey research, the questionnaire would more likely be used to quantify issues. For example, the questionnaire might be used to find out what percentage of people have particular viewpoints. Data probably would be analyzed

Figure 4.4. Needs Analysis Methods

Method	Examples
• Observation	Observe a trained flight attendant demonstrate in-flight safety procedures.
• Questionnaires	Send questionnaire to country oil company depot managers.
• Interviews	Conduct telephone interviews with a sample of bank accountants in the metropolitan area.
• Tests	Test problem-solving ability of all new plumbing apprentices.
• Workshop Techniques	Arrange for administrative officers to meet in a group and brainstorm the training and educational needs of clerical staff during the next five years.
• Field Notes	Each time you visit the plant, make notes straight afterward. These should record what happened, your impressions, new information, and follow-up actions that are needed.
• Photographs or Videotapes	Phtotograph or videotape each section of a production line in operation, and use these records in discussion with workers and management to examine problems.
• Assessment of Products or Services	Examine a committee of enquiry's report on a recent trucking accident to determine possible training needs.
• Productivity Measures	Compare productivity and error rates among different process workers.
• Performance Appraisal	Collate and analyze performance appraisal data.
• Document Analysis	Analyze any relevant written information: letters of complaint, minutes of meetings, correspondence, union circulars, or personnel files.
• Steering Committee	Set up a committee of data-entry workers to help plan and implement initiatives related to training.

Investigate Skills and Training Issues

solely by the researcher and typically would be presented in a written form to management and perhaps employees.

Analyze Tasks

The trainer may need to obtain a description of the steps that are involved in each competency. This information can be used to perform the following tasks:

- Prepare competency guides, sometimes called *job sheets;*
- Prepare instructional materials and manuals;
- Train trainers in how to use, and ultimately show others how to use, new equipment; and
- Develop or check assessment materials.

One way of investigating a particular competency is to observe a skilled employee. As discussed in Chapter 2, a competency that consists of a routine sequence of steps is called a *task*. Therefore, research into routine competencies that involves direct observation is often called *task analysis*. There are many task-analysis methods but all of these are related to one of the two approaches discussed in the following paragraphs.

Simple Task Analysis

In this approach, the main actions involved in each task are analyzed without attempting to record every detail. Typically, a simple task analysis would involve discussions with skilled employees, either individually or in a group. These could be combined with visits to the work site to observe the demonstration of the task. The information collected might include a list of the steps associated with the task and any important points that a learner needs to be made aware of. This information would be recorded on a form called a *competency guide* (Figure 4.5).

Figure 4.5. Sample Competency Guide

	Section system B 163	Document number 9-13
	Competency LOAD ROADTANKER FROM B163	
STAGE	**STEPS**	**KEY POINTS**
Prepare tanker for loading	• MSA the tanker • Driver to position the tanker into loading bay 3 • Place chocks under front and back wheels • Connect each strap to tanker • Driver to connect liquid and vapor hose from truck to spout 5 • Driver to open liquid and vapor isolation valves and vent the interspaces between tanker and spout isolation valves • **If tanker has been carrying on spec C4s:** Connect vapor to B163 • **If C4s have not been carried:** Shut vapor valve to B163 and open up route to flare	Driver must switch off engine and apply handbrake This step removes air in pipes Check previous tanker contents with driver
Check that J173 is ready	• Open shand and jurs valve, and pump up to maximum pressure • Check C4 route through the filter	

Investigate Skills and Training Issues

Once a competency guide has been drafted, it needs to be edited. The editing process might consist of checking for the following:

Clarity. Remove vague and easily misunderstood words.

Completeness. Make sure the competency guide contains all the necessary information, including, if applicable, particular tools or equipment. Avoid abbreviations unless they are widely known.

Conciseness. Check that current occupational terms are used. Use a consistent format for the wording of each section of the competency guide.

The trainer will want to verify the information at this stage. This might be done by giving a copy of the draft to an experienced employee or technical expert to review. The reviewer typically would be asked to check the accuracy of the information and to modify steps or key points as necessary.

Detailed Task Analysis

The trainer may find it necessary to analyze a competency or task in great detail. This might happen when the activity:

- Involves unusual cues or movements;
- Is done incorrectly often; and
- Is not well understood by the trainer or employees.

In detailed task analysis, an attempt is made to record every detail of behavior and decision making (Figure 4.6). A skilled employee might be asked to perform a task many times; video might be used to record the minute details. During the repetitions of the task, the trainer might ask questions about why certain responses were made and what the employee was paying attention to.

Figure 4.6. Example of a Detailed Task Analysis [6]

JOB DESCRIPTION: Assemble base (See sketches of parts and layout)			REF:		
^			SHEET No. *1* of *1*		
^			ANALYST:		
^			DATE:		
LEFT-HAND DESCRIPTION	LH	TMU	RH	RIGHT-HAND DESCRIPTION	
Get base from box.	GC30	23	G—	Get pin from box.	
		14	GC5	^	
Put base on bench.	PA30	30	PC30	Locate pin to base.	
Get block from box.	GC30	23	G—	Get stud from box.	
		14	GC5	^	
Move block stud.	P—	30	PC30	Locate stud through block.	
Assist location.	P—	26	PC15	Fit assembly to base.	
		23	GC30	Get connector from box.	
Assist location.	GB—	30	PC30	Locate to stud.	

The thinking behind detailed task analysis can be traced back to Frederic Taylor, whose investigations resulted in an approach called "time-and-motion" study. Detailed task analysis is one form of time-and-motion study. Such methods have only limited applications in the training field because they are out of step with current thinking in areas like industrial relations and because many of the skills needed in modern industries are under the surface and, therefore, difficult to analyze by direct observation.

End Notes

1. See Fuller, Oxley, and Hayton (1988).

2. Margo Pearson, from ANU, helped me appreciate the superficiality of some of the needs assessment theory.

3. Adapted from Kemmis (1982). Copyright 1988 Deakin University. Reprinted with permission.

4. Based in part on Fuller, Oxley, and Hayton (1988).

5. Derived from work done by the author for ICI, and used with the company's permission.

6. Taken from the ILO publication, Introduction to Work Study (1979) and used with permission.

Bibliography

Charner, I., & Rolzinski, C. (Eds.). (1987, Spring). *Responding to the educational needs of today's workplace* (Higher Education Sourcebook Series No. 33). San Francisco, CA: Jossey-Bass.

Cohen, L., & Manion, L. (1980). *Research methods in education.* London: Croom Helm.

Fuller, D., Oxley, G., & Hayton, S. (1988). *Training for Australian industry.* Canberra, Australia: Australian Government Publishing Service.

Gael, S. (1983). *Job analysis: A guide to assessing work activities.* San Francisco, CA: Jossey-Bass.

Kemmis, S. (1982). *The action research planner.* Waurn Ponds, Australia: Deakin University.

Marsick, V., & Watkins, K. (1907). Approaches to studying learning in the workplace. In V. Marsick (Ed.), *Learning in the workplace.* London: Croom Helm.

Martin, P., & Nicholls, J. (1987). *Creating a committed workforce.* London: Institute of Personnel Management.

Reeves, T., & Harper, D. (1981). *Surveys at work - A practitioner's guide.* London: McGraw-Hill.

Ulschak, F. (1983). *Human resource development: The theory and practice of need assessment.* Reston, U.S.A.: Reston Publishing.

Zemke, R., & Kramlinger, T. (1981). *Figuring things out: A trainer's guide to needs and task analysis.* Reading, MA: Addison-Wesley.

Zemke, R. et al. (1981). *Designing and delivering cost-effective training.* Minneapolis, MN: Lakewood Publications.

An ideal way to assess competence is to observe the employee as he or she works

Analyze Job Competencies

In recent years, there has been a trend toward competency-based training in many countries. Employers, unions, and many governments are all keen to see vocational programs that are more job related, more effective, and better integrated with various other areas of workplace improvement, such as new technology and a more flexible industrial-relations framework. The competency-based training approach is viewed as a way to help achieve these ends.

For these reasons, trainers are hearing more about competency-based training, and some are directly involved in preparing competency profiles (Figure 5.1) or in redesigning programs around competencies.

This chapter covers some of the features of competency-based training. It describes the characteristics of this approach and looks at its advantages and limitations. Chapter 5 also discusses the steps involved in setting up a competency-based training program.

Competency-Based Training Program

Although not all competency-based training programs are structured in exactly the same way, most have the characteristics listed on pages 83 and 85.

Figure 5-1. Part of a Competency Profile for a Draftsperson[1]

COMPETENCY AREA	COMPETENCIES						
A Conduct Field Work	A-1 Take Measurements	A-2 Determine Site Orientation	A-3 Make Site Inspections	A-4 Use Surveying Techniques	A-5 Develop Working Sketches		
B Develop Preliminary Studies and Presentations	B-1 Prepare Rough Sketches	B-2 Prepare Preliminary Drawings	B-3 Make Models	B-4 Prepare Presentation Drawings			
C Prepare Final Drawings	C-1 Determine Type and Size of Medium	C-2 Attach Medium to Board	C-3 Prepare Surface for Drawing	C-4 Determine Details to be Shown (Isometric)	C-5 Lay Drawings	C-6 Select and Use Appropriate Line Weights	C-7 Draw Detail Views
D Prepare Written Documents	D-1 Develop Written Instructions	D-2 Generate Job Orders	D-3 Write Change Orders	D-4 Submit Requisitions for Drafting Supplies	D-5 Submit Requisitions for Services	D-6 Develop Inputs for Contracts	D-7 Prepare Memos and Letters
E Check Drawings	E-1 Check Accuracy of Dimensions and Scale	E-2 Check Coordination of Prints	E-3 Check Revisions	E-4 Check for Completeness	E-5 Check Line Quality	E-6 Verify Compliance with Building Codes	E-7 Check Clarity of Notes
F Maintain Document Storage	F-1 File Masters	F-2 File Media Materials	F-3 Retrieve Media and Masters	F-4 Maintain File of Revisions	F-5 Maintain Drawing Log		

Program content is based directly on the skills needed to perform a job. The competencies that have to be mastered by employees are worked out in advance using analytical methods like those described in Chapter 4. The main purpose of using these methods is to find out what the job consists of. Just because an employee regularly spends time performing an activity, the trainer cannot assume that this activity is a competency. The trainer will need to find out whether the activity is necessary to perform the job well.

Performance objectives are written for each competency statement. Competency statements are often phrased in general terms and, on their own, are not usually specific enough to be used for training. To make them more meaningful, trainers will have to list details about how each competency should be performed. Such a list might include the conditions surrounding an activity and the performance standards. The activity, conditions, and performance standards associated with each competency are often combined and expressed as a performance objective.

Figure 5.2 shows how a general bank-teller's job can be dissected into competencies. It also shows how performance objectives can be written for a typical competency of a general bank teller.

Skills assessment is based on demonstrated competence. Employees are assessed as objectively as possible using the most realistic situations available. The ideal way to assess competence is to observe the employee as he or she performs the task in the work environment.

Employee performance is assessed by means of criterion-referenced measures. In a criterion-referenced assessment, an employee must meet a predetermined standard. Each employee's performance is compared to this standard rather than to other employees' assessment results. Often, in competency-

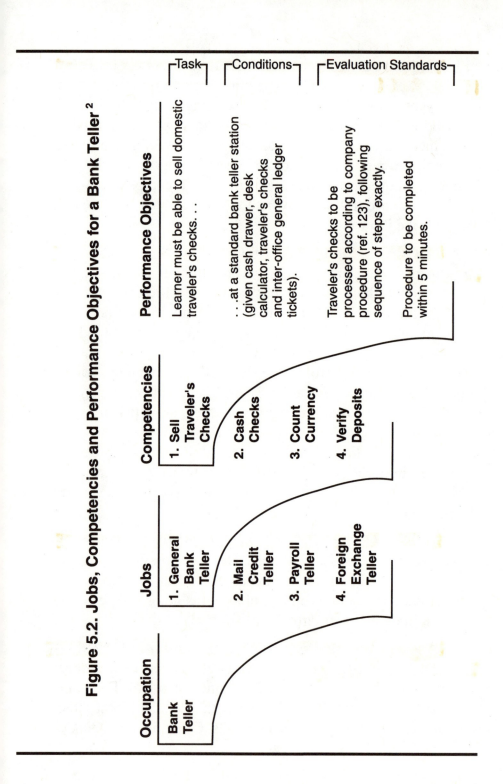

Figure 5.2. Jobs, Competencies and Performance Objectives for a Bank Teller [2]

based training, the standard is to perform the activity "without any errors."

A complete record of achievement of competencies is developed for each employee. Each employee's achievements, in terms of competencies, are recorded on a printed report or computer document. In some training programs, such a record could be many pages long. A copy of this record is given to the employee, and another copy is kept by the trainer conducting the program.

In addition to these essential aspects of competency-based training, training programs of this type often have some or all of the following characteristics:

Individualized materials are used. Typically, employees would be given workbooks designed to help them learn the competency or group of competencies. Individualized competency-based programs sometimes require computers or other instructional media, such as laser videodiscs.

Learning time is flexible. In a competency-based program, a trainer can accommodate the various backgrounds, needs, and abilities of the employees by letting them work at their own pace. This is particularly helpful for employees who are inexperienced or take longer to learn than others as well as for those who quickly master the competency and want to move on to new areas. Such an approach requires careful management and adequate resources if it is to work smoothly.

Learning is guided by feedback. Training programs should be structured in such a way that feedback about skill acquisition is provided regularly. For example, checklists and other reference materials may guide the employees' initial attempts to perform the competency. Quizzes and skill tests that employees can mark themselves are also often included in competency-based programs.

Advantages and Limitations of Competency-Based Training

There have been many advantages claimed for applying the competency-based training approach to in-house training. It has been found that competency-based training can do the following:

- Give each employee enough time to master each competency before moving on to the next one;
- Shorten training time for some employees;
- Effectively meet the needs of employees who learn very slowly or very quickly;
- Increase the likelihood that employees will do well in a course, which can reduce absenteeism, tardiness, attrition rates, and behavior problems within the organization;
- Make it possible for educational institutions to offer open-entry, open-exit, self-paced programs;
- Allow performance standards to be constant and at a high level and allow individual training time to vary;
- Enable employees who enjoy the challenge and freedom to take responsibility for their own learning;
- Encourage greater accountability of both employees and trainers;
- Result in more effective articulation among educational institutions and between them and the workplace, because of the availability of clear competency statements; and

- Keep employees task oriented and active.

Limitations to competency-based training need to be taken into account. For example, this approach tends to:

- Focus very much on the current job and, thus, downplay the need for broad-based skills or technological skills;
- Assume that once an employee is competent, he or she remains competent; and
- Overemphasize specific areas that can be divided into self-contained, observable tasks and ignore areas such as employees' pride in their work.

This last point is very important and it is illustrated by the following example. Two different competencies that might be needed by employees in an engineering company could be the following:

- Assemble standard bolted joints and components; and
- Show initiative by identifying ways of improving work efficiency and increasing productivity.

The first competency is a routine activity that could easily be dealt with in training. In terms of the skills-iceberg model, it uses skills that are mainly above the surface. The second competency, which could be just as important or even more important for adequate job performance, is more difficult and perhaps impossible to cover in a formal training program.

The second competency would also be hard to assess. The danger in using competency-based training is that too much attention is given to routine activities like the one in the first example and too little attention is given to skills like the one in the second example.

Setting Up a Competency-Based Training Program

In order to set up a competency-based training program, whether it is within a company or department, across an industry, or within a specific teaching area, a trainer needs to answer the following questions:

- What does *competence* mean for this project?
- How will terms like *skill, job, task,* and *competency* be used?
- What group is being targeted?
- What is the competency profile of a capable employee?
- Are the competencies properly expressed?
- How should the competencies be grouped?
- Are the competencies valid?
- Can each competency be taught?

The next section looks at some of the things that a trainer needs to take into account in order to answer each question.

Question 1: What does *competence* mean for this project?

The trainer has to decide how he or she will know that an employee is competent and make sure that the definition decided on is shared by others, including management. Following are three examples of the meaning of competence:

Example 1: Competence will be taken to mean the ability to perform activities safely and to the minimum acceptable standard without supervision.

Example 2: To be certified as competent, an employee must perform each activity twice with approximately four weeks between each attempt. An employee may refer to the component manual but must otherwise work without assistance. No errors are allowed.

Example 3: For routine tasks, competence will be assessed by the employee's ability to follow the steps laid out in the competency guide and to answer questions about the procedure. All other competencies will be judged by a joint committee comprising one management representative and two experienced employees. Competencies other than routine tasks will be rated on a four-point scale.

Question 2: How will terms like *skill, job, task,* and *competency* be used?

Chapter 2 defined each of these terms and showed how they relate to one another. Unless the trainer has good reasons for using the terms differently—for example, if some of the terms are already widely used in different ways within an industry and change is likely to cause confusion—it is suggested that this terminology be used. But the main thing is that the trainer establish agreed-on meanings for key terms as early in the project as possible.

Question 3: What group is being targeted?

The trainer needs to decide what group or groups he or she is interested in. Following are examples:

- Experienced technicians
- Probationary police
- Clerical personnel

Writing a brief list of groups like this one helps to clarify who is included in the target group and who is not included.

Question 4: What is the competency profile of a capable employee?

Create a profile of a competent employee. The competency profile is the foundation of a competency-based training program. The trainer needs to work through this stage carefully. Typically, the following two things need to be done at the same time:

Collect written information. Collect any written information that is available on the target group. Consult documents such as reports by unions, employer groups, and so on. Find out about previous courses that the target group attended and look for information about any other attempts to investigate the skills that the group needs.

Consult employees. Set up a small committee of employees who can do the job well and work with the committee to build up the competency profile (Figure 5.3).

Question 5: Are the competencies properly expressed?

After drafting a list of competencies, the trainer will need to edit them. This might involve the following:

- Editing descriptions for greater precision;
- Breaking down some competency statements into more specific ones;
- Making up additional statements;
- Deleting or combining statements; and
- Moving competencies from one area to another.

Make sure that the competencies are all expressed in the same way. For example, each competency can be expressed as a simple statement of activity that begins with a verb (Figure 5.4).

Figure 5.3. Competency Profile for Probationary Police

To draw up a competency profile for probationary police, a group of police with experience in a wide range of duties worked together for more than a week. The profile was produced in stages, like this:

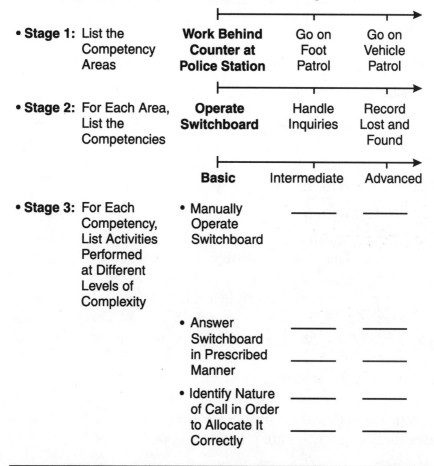

- **Stage 1:** List the Competency Areas — **Work Behind Counter at Police Station** | Go on Foot Patrol | Go on Vehicle Patrol

- **Stage 2:** For Each Area, List the Competencies — **Operate Switchboard** | Handle Inquiries | Record Lost and Found

- **Stage 3:** For Each Competency, List Activities Performed at Different Levels of Complexity

	Basic	Intermediate	Advanced
• Manually Operate Switchboard		___	___
• Answer Switchboard in Prescribed Manner		___	___
• Identify Nature of Call in Order to Allocate It Correctly		___	___

Question 6: How should the competencies be grouped?

Group the competencies in some logical way. This can be done with the help of the committee as part of the checking process. Figure 5.5 shows some of the ways that competencies can be grouped.

Figure 5.4. Editing Competency Lists

Draft Version	▶	Edited Version
To Monitor Levels of VC		Monitor VC Levels
Gas Detectors/Testing		Use Gas Detectors for Testing
Management of Storage Tanks		Manage Storage Tanks

Question 7: Are the competencies valid?

The group that writes the competency profile cannot be expected to represent all the views about skills needed in a job or occupation. There may be differences related to work location or various specialties that result in the need to include different competencies. It is also possible that the committee could make mistakes. The validation process is a way of checking such possibilities and making sure that the competency profile is accurate.

During the validation process, the trainer normally asks a cross section of experienced practitioners to check that the competencies listed are the ones needed to perform the job and that the competencies are properly grouped.

Question 8: Can this competency be taught?

Many competencies that are important in doing jobs probably cannot be taught, and it helps the trainer to be realistic about the limits of training. If the answer to the question "Can this competency be taught?" is yes, the trainer needs to think about

Figure 5.5. Ways of Grouping Competencies

- **By Complexity**

Basic Competencies	Intermediate Competencies	Advanced Competencies
_____	_____	_____
_____	_____	_____
_____	_____	_____

- **By Assessment Standard**

Essential (100% Test Result Required)	Important (80% Test Result Required)
_____	_____
_____	_____
_____	_____

- **By Location**

Competencies Needed to Work in Seciton A (or on System Z)	Competencies Needed to Work in Division A (or Plant Z)	Competencies Needed to Work Anywhere in Organization (or Across Site)
_____	_____	_____
_____	_____	_____
_____	_____	_____

  Competencies for the Retail Industry

- **By Industry Sector**

Common	Food	Electrical	Hardware
_____	_____	_____	_____
_____	_____	_____	_____
_____	_____	_____	_____

- **By Level at Which Competency Is Needed**

Storeman	Junior Sales Assistant	Senior Sales Assistant	Assistant Manager
_____	_____	_____	_____
_____	_____	_____	_____
_____	_____	_____	_____

- **By Job Classification**

Common to All Tellers	Savings Only	Trading Only
_____	_____	_____
_____	_____	_____
_____	_____	_____

Analyze Job Competencies

the ways in which training might be offered. These could include a combination of some of the following approaches:

- On-the-job training under the guidance of a supervisor or experienced employee;
- A formal training program administered by an external organization;
- Using self-directed learning modules;
- Computer-aided learning;
- Formal in-house classroom training; or
- Simulator training.

On the other hand, if the answer to the question is no, then other strategies such as changing employees' incentives, recruiting new employees, or introducing job rotation may have to be considered.

End Notes

1. Adapted from material obtained from the American Association for Vocational Instructional Materials.
2. Based in part on Bortz (1981).

Bibliography

Bortz, R. (1981). *Handbook for developing occupational curricula.* Boston, MA: Allyn and Bacon.

Christie, R. (1985). Training for competence: The nature and assessment of the beast. *Journal of European Industrial Training, 9,* 6, 30-32.

Davis, R., Alexander, L., & Yelon, S. (1974). *Learning system design.* New York: McGraw-Hill.

Hawke, G. (1988). *Competency testing in NSW.* Sydney: NSW Department of TAFE.

Horne, R. (1982). *Guide for implementing competency-based education in vocational programs*. Blacksburg, VA: Virginia Department of Education, Division of Vocational and Adult Education.

Romiszowski, A. (1984). *Producing instructional systems*. London: Kogan Page.

A *performance objective states an activity and how it is to be assessed*

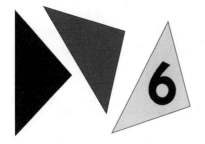

State Performance Objectives

Performance objectives consist of a statement about an action, conditions under which the action is performed, and assessment standards. Following are two examples:

- Assemble a bookcase using a diagram of the bookcase and the instruction manual. Complete the assembly within thirty minutes and without errors.
- Using standard labels, load a pricing gun within thirty seconds.

Performance objectives are very useful in training, especially when tasks are involved. However, despite their usefulness in many types of skills training and despite the fact that they are widely advocated in the vocational-education literature, performance objectives are not appropriate for every type of training.

Chapter 6 looks at performance objectives and discusses the correct ways to write them. The chapter then examines their applications and limitations and provides a number of hints for writing and using performance objectives effectively.

Stating Performance Objectives

A performance objective is a clear statement of what activities the employee should be able to perform and how to measure those activities. The approach recommended for writing performance objectives is shown in Figure 6.1.

Figure 6.1. Standard Format for Performance Objectives

	Activity	+ Condition	+ Standard
Learners should be able to…	load a pricing gun	using standard labels	within 30 seconds.
Learners should be able to…	label the parts of a rotary engine	given an unlabeled diagram	without error.
Learners should be able to…	answer incoming telephone calls	using the approved company greeting and call procedure	so that there are no cut-offs and all calls are connected within 10 seconds.

The following section explains each part of the performance objective in more detail.

Activity

Write the activity that the employee should be able to perform by the end of the training session—not what the trainer intends to achieve in the training room. Use clear, unambiguous wording that reflects the type of activity that the objective refers to.

Following are examples of how to phrase the activity portion of a performance objective:

- Locate problems in a circuit.
- Measure a patient's blood pressure.
- Handle a complaint made by a customer.
- Use an insulation tester.

The verb in an activity statement should refer to a training outcome. Training outcomes are often classified into the following three groups:

- Knowledge
- Physical activity
- Attitude

Figure 6.2 lists some useful words for describing training outcomes that fit into each group.

Figure 6.2. Useful Words to Use When Writing Performance Objectives

Type of Outcome	Meaning	Sample Words	
Knowledge	Related to thinking, knowing, understanding, and perceiving.	Define State List Identify	Describe Estimate Classify Evaluate
Physical Activity	Related to actions and the way they are performed.	Adjust Tune Measure Replace	Construct Assemble Open Insert
Attitude	Related to feelings, values, personality, and character.	Accept Monitor Develop Coordinate	Empathize Influence Associate Change

State Performance Objectives

Conditions

State the conditions associated with the competency. The conditions could include any aspects of the environment in which the competency is performed, such as tools, job aids, equipment, lighting, space restrictions, or customer pressures. Examples of conditions that might be included in an objective are as follows:

- During a storm;
- Given all necessary tools, test equipment, and documentation;
- Without assistance;
- Using a calculator and a set of traveler's checks; and
- Using a word processor.

Standards

State the standards of competent performance. These should be based on workplace standards and each employee's ability. For example, the trainer should take into account whether the employee is just beginning a job, or if he or she is very experienced. Standards can be numerical or descriptive:

- Within .005 mm;
- With no more than one error per trial;
- In the order specified in the manual; and
- Without any errors.

As Figure 6.3 indicates, there are three types of standards:

- Preparation
- Process
- Product

Figure 6.3. Types of Performance Standards

Type of Standard	Example from Hairdressing Trade
Preparation: Checking diagnosis and use of correct tools.	To determine the base color, texture, and condition of hair prior to coloring.
Process: The way the task is performed, the sequence for doing each step, and the time taken.	To apply the correct amount of hair dye according to the texture and porosity of the hair and the desired result.
Product: The size, shape, and standard of the finished job.	To achieve an even, finished tint.

Uses and Limitations of Performance Objectives

Performance objectives are widely advocated in the vocational-education literature, and there are a number of benefits in using them. For example, performance objectives give training sessions a better focus and make assessments more meaningful. When employees are told what the performance objectives are for each session, they are likely to feel less anxious, more confident, and better able to direct their own learning.

Despite these benefits, the worth of performance objectives is sometimes overrated, and many trainers do not strictly follow the action plus conditions plus standards approach to planning training. The following page lists some reasons for the difference between what is advocated and what actually happens in practice:

- Performance objectives work well with routine tasks, physical activities, and the learning of factual information, but, as Chapter 2 explained, activities such as these account for only a small proportion of the skills needed by employees. Performance objectives are not very useful when a training course deals with under-the-surface skills such as teamwork, problem solving, and system monitoring. As the level of technology in the workplace increases, it is possible that performance objectives will be used less and less often.

- Although performance objectives are supposed to be written in such a way that conditions and standards link closely to the workplace, what commonly happens in practice is that this link is weak or even nonexistent. Consider, for example, this ideal performance objective from a recent publication:

    Given a bin of assorted electrical components and the request to "sort out the resistors from the capacitors," the employee will be able to identify resistors and capacitors by selecting them from the bin and putting them into separate piles. No reference materials will be used, and the employee will complete the sorting at a rate of fifteen pieces per minute.

It is unlikely that the conditions and standards in this example correspond closely to any competencies needed on the job.

Too often the trainer writes performance objectives mainly for his or her own convenience, thereby neglecting workplace training needs. The tendency to be pedantic and overly behavioristic has unfortunately come to be associated with performance objectives, and this has probably limited their acceptance in industrial training.

Hints for Writing Useful Performance Objectives[1]

Despite the limitations of performance objectives, they do have many applications in vocational education, if they are used with flexibility and common sense. This section offers suggestions for using performance objectives effectively:

- Use performance objectives only for appropriate skill areas. Use them for self-contained, routine physical tasks, and for job-related knowledge, but think twice about using them for training dealing with attitudes, motivation, handling customers, problem solving, and self-development. For skill areas like the latter, the trainer probably cannot plan detailed outcomes or performance standards in any meaningful way. Instead, training sessions should be structured around activities that learners can participate in and use in ways that benefit them. Training in these areas should also be sufficiently flexible so that participants can have a role in planning how their time will be spent.

- Use lists to avoid repetition. Instead of using the following instructions:

    a. Given a customer's bank card, withdraw funds as requested according to standard bank procedure (ref. ABC).

    b. Given a customer's MasterCard, withdraw funds as requested according to standard bank procedure (ref. XYZ).

    Consolidate the instructions into a simpler format, such as the following:

    Withdraw funds as requested according to standard bank procedures from:

State Performance Objectives ♦ *103*

a. Bank card (ref. Procedure ABC)

b. MasterCard (ref. Procedure XYZ)

- Get rid of any unnecessary words, such as the following:

  <u>For learners to be able</u> to <u>correctly</u> take a reading using an Ajax gas detector.

  (No need to say each time) (can be assumed)

  An improved version of the sentence is given below:

  Take a reading using an Ajax gas detector.

- If conditions or standards are constant, do not repeat them. Often conditions or standards will be the same for a group of objectives. There is no need to keep repeating the same information for each; simply stating it once—on an information sheet or in a workbook, for example—is sufficient.

- Use several sentences to break up long objectives. Instead of stating the objectives in the following manner:

  Given all necessary tools, test equipment, and documentation, perform all necessary adjustments on a functioning but maladjusted engine.

  State the objectives in this manner:

  Perform all necessary adjustments on a functioning but maladjusted engine. You will be supplied with all necessary tools, test equipment, and documentation.

- Do not make up artificial conditions or standards. In some situations, performance conditions and assessment standards are well-known to both trainers and employees. Do not create conditions or standards just to fit into the performance-objective format. Simply leave out the unnecessary parts of the objective.

End Note

1. Based in part on Heines (1980) and Lewis (1981).

Bibliography

Clark, D. (1972). *Using instructional objectives in teaching*. Glenview, IL: Scott, Foresman.

Corwell, J. (1981, January). Measure trainees against objectives before you train them. *Training/HRD*.

Davis, R., Alexander, L., & Yelon, S. (1974). *Learning system design*. New York: McGraw-Hill.

Heines, J. (1980, July). Writing objectives with style. *Training/HRD*.

Lewis, J. (1981, March). The whens, whys and hows of behavioural objectives. *Training/HRD*.

Mager, R. (1975). *Preparing instructional objectives*. Belmont, CA: Fearon.

Romiszowski, A. (1984). *Producing instructional systems*. London: Kogan Page.

Steele, S., & Brack, R. (1973). *Evaluating the attainment of objectives in adult education: Process, properties, problems and prospects*. Syracuse, NY: Syracuse University, Publications in Continuing Education.

Make sure the information in user manuals is easily accessible

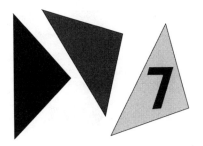

Design and Use Job Aids[1]

The term "job aid" covers a range of materials and technology that make it easier for employees to perform a competency. Job aids can be very valuable. They can solve workplace problems without the need for training or they may simply be used to supplement training or other measures. In some circumstances, job aids may also be inappropriate, so it is worth understanding their limitations, too.

Chapter 7 examines some of the factors that determine whether job aids are needed to support skilled work. It also discusses and provides examples of the three most common types of job aids: job-reference guides, technical-user manuals, and on-line job aids (Figure 7.1).

Is a Job Aid Needed?

To decide whether a job aid is appropriate, consider the following factors:

Is the work environment suitable? If job aids are not located near the work itself, then they need to be relocated to the place where the work is being done. For example, set the job aid on a counter or beside a machine. Employees need to be able to refer to them easily. "Paper" aids, that is, job-reference guides and

Figure 7.1. Types of Job Aids

- **Job Reference Guides:** These include cards, charts, or brief printed documents that contain in summary form some of the information needed to complete a task.

- **Technical User Manuals:** These include manuals dealing with operating, manufacturing or processing systems, fault-finding, and the use of data bases and software.

- **On-Line Job Aids:** These include a variety of computer-linked job aids, such as help screens, procedural cues, and menus.

user manuals, may need to be protected from chemicals and other corrosive substances, and they may have to withstand rough treatment.

Is the job compatible with using a job aid? Job aids are mainly suited to competencies that meet the following criteria:

- Are complex;
- Involve many steps;
- Are not changed very often;

- Involve a routine sequence;
- Have serious consequences if done incorrectly; and
- Are often done incorrectly.

Will employees refer to it? Job aids will not contribute to solving workplace problems unless they are used, and that means that the organizational culture must be such that employees do not feel embarrassed about using job aids. It also suggests that the aids must be designed in such a way that they correspond to employees' educational levels and language skills.

Does the job involve elements that suggest a job aid is inappropriate? A job aid might not be appropriate if the following statements are true:

- Employees have little or no say over their work pace. Job aids require that employees have time to stop and refer to them.
- The task involves steps that employees are required to memorize.
- The task involves estimating, acting on hunches, and deciding among numerous options.
- The task involves terminology that is new to employees and that would be difficult to explain in a job aid.
- Employees need a good understanding of the task before they perform it.

Job-Reference Guides

Types of Job-Reference Guides

The first category of job aids that will be discussed in this chapter is job-reference guides, which consist of cards, charts, or brief printed documents that contain the information needed to perform a task or group of tasks. The three types of job-reference guides commonly used are as follows:

- Those that list a sequence of step-by-step activities;
- Those that make it easier to record information or to perform calculations; and
- Those that help employees to identify faulty products or procedural errors.

Preparing a Job-Reference Guide[2]

Designing an effective job-reference guide is not as straightforward as it might seem. Following are some suggestions about how to design one:

Study how the guide will be used. Talk with the intended users and become familiar with their problems and needs before settling on a reference guide as a solution.

Get expert help. If there are people who have experience with the equipment or system for which the guide is being developed, involve them in working out what the needed information is. If the guide deals with new technology, ask for help from the suppliers.

Put only what is necessary in the guide. Make sure the guide contains enough information to be clear, but do not include unnecessary words. (Put more detailed information in manuals that employees can refer to when necessary.)

Avoid ambiguous quantities. Make sure that references to any numerical information, such as time, size, mass, or frequency, are specific. For example, "Dip tank after it has been off-line for at least two hours."

List the activities in the sequence in which they happen. For example, instead of writing "Push the button when the pump stops," write "When the pump stops, push the button."

Use boldface type for key words. Any words that need to be emphasized should be set in boldface type. For example, "Shut off vacuum supply **before** turning machine by hand."

Use diagrams if appropriate. Diagrams help to simplify explanations (Figure 7.2). They are particularly useful if the employees speak a different language, if there is a need to distinguish between several conditions or products, or if the orientation of components is important.

Design the reference guide to suit the job environment. The reference guide must be easy to refer to if it is to be useful.

Figure 7.2. Use of Simple Diagrams in a Job-Reference Guide

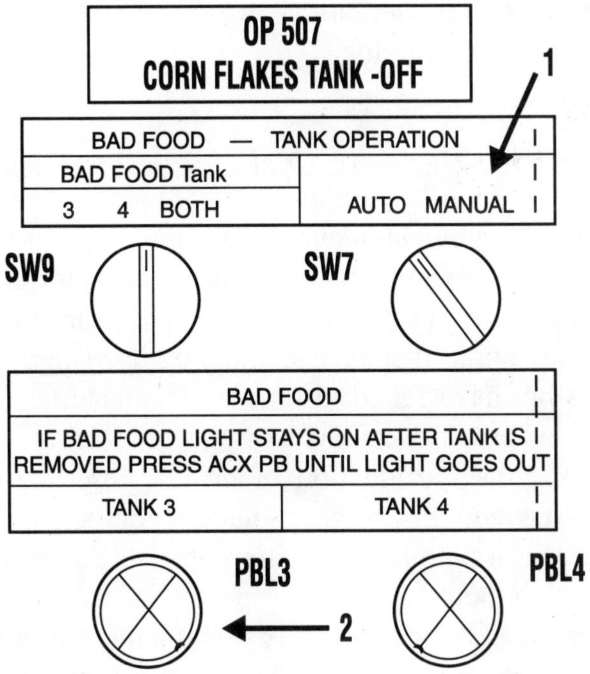

```
              OP 507
          CORN FLAKES TANK -OFF        1
       ┌──────────────────┬──────────────┐
       │ BAD FOOD — TANK OPERATION      │
       │ BAD FOOD Tank    │              │
       │  3   4   BOTH    │ AUTO  MANUAL │
       └──────────────────┴──────────────┘
    SW9                SW7

       ┌──────────────────────────────────┐
       │            BAD FOOD              │
       │ IF BAD FOOD LIGHT STAYS ON AFTER │
       │ TANK IS REMOVED PRESS ACX PB     │
       │ UNTIL LIGHT GOES OUT             │
       │    TANK 3       │    TANK 4      │
       └─────────────────┴────────────────┘
         PBL3                    PBL4
              ← 2
```

Design and Use Job Aids

Design it so that the employees will understand the information and they will be able to find information easily.

Have the employees test the guide. Create a mock-up of the guide before having it printed, and try it out on-site with employees of different abilities. Incorporate the improvements that are suggested.

Technical-User Manuals

A second type of "paper" job aid is a technical-user manual. This document contains instructions about how to operate a system or how to manage a process. A technical-user manual is widely used in jobs involving computer-integrated systems and other complex technical equipment. In training approaches that rely on self-directed learning, all relevant technical information needs to be made available in an accessible format to the employees. In some cases, adequate documentation can replace the need for formal training.

The Need for Adequate User Documentation

Unfortunately, technical documentation in many organizations is haphazard or even nonexistent. This problem is not restricted to organizations using old technology. There are many examples of organizations that have recently updated their equipment or systems but have failed to provide adequate technical-user manuals. This problem can even occur across whole industries. For example, the introduction of on-line reservations in the travel industry could have been much smoother if travel consultants had been supplied with comprehensive manuals and had been trained in their use.

Systems can be inadequately documented for a variety of reasons:

- No one in the organization has the time or experience to document the system.

- The technology was imported and because of differences in language and technoculture, the manuals that were provided by the supplier are unsuited to the requirements of the country in which they are to be used.

For reasons like these, trainers may need to be involved in producing user manuals. However, a word of caution is needed. Manuals can take an enormous amount of time to write, and the trainer's involvement has to be weighed against his or her other work priorities. Manual preparation may well come within another department's responsibilities, such as the computer or information-systems department. Manuals also may be written under the supervision of systems experts by technical writers who are employed on a freelance basis.

Structuring User Documentation

When preparing a technical-user manual, keep in mind who will be using it. The manual should be written in clear, simple language and designed so that it can easily be referred to. A user manual rarely is meant to be a complete technical digest. Its main purpose is to provide concise, direct information about a particular process or piece of equipment and to give clear, step-by-step directions.

Another important point about preparing a manual is that the writer should start by thinking about the user, not the system or its design principles. The ways that an engineer or computer-software expert views the structure of a plant or computer system do not necessarily coincide with the needs of those who have to work in the plant or use the software. For this reason, system users as well as system designers should be involved in the preparation of the manual.

Although it is outside the scope of this book to discuss different types of user manuals in detail, it might be helpful to look briefly at one effective way of structuring a manual. This approach was used for a series of operator-reference manuals prepared for a chemical-processing plant. Figure 7.3 shows how each manual was structured, and Figure 7.4 shows examples of the two page formats that were most frequently used.

Steps in the Production of a Technical Manual

The steps typically involved in writing a technical manual are as follows:

1. *Research the topic.* Collect as much relevant information as possible. As the information is collected, try to sort out where it will be placed in the finished manual. Talk to people who have particular knowledge of the section, system, or equipment for which the manual is being written. Find out if any training materials have recently been produced on this subject. Determine how current the collected information is.

2. *Prepare the first draft.* Sort the material you have collected into sections: structure, safety, jobs, and so on. Use the page-format guidelines shown in Figure 7.4 to help structure the material. The first draft might contain a combination of handwritten material, amended photocopies, and edited diagrams; in other words, it can be quite rough at this stage.

3. *Edit and type the manual.* Have the first draft typed on a word processor. Arrange to have technical drawings modified or produced and flow charts drawn. Diagrams can range from fine 3-D drawings produced on a CAD system to photos with hand-drawn labels. Often fairly

Figure 7.3. An Approach to Structuring an Operator-Reference Manual[3]

1. **Introduction:** Provide a map and photos to indicate the location and main features of the system.

2. **Overview:** Provide an overview of the whole system and describe its purpose. Explain the basic process in simple terms, with accompanying stylized process diagrams. Describe the arrangement of the system and show the location of this part of the plant in relation to other parts.

3. **Normal Operations of the System:** Describe the normal operations of this system. Where appropriate, indicate if other parts of the manual (such as the competency guides) provide more detailed information.

4. **Competency Guides:** Indicate step by step what is involved in each of the competencies for this system. In these guides, draw attention to any difficult, dangerous, or particularly critical steps.

5. **Abnormal Operations of the System:** Provide details of all abnormal operations.

6. **Equipment:** Give details of the equipment in this system. If appropriate, describe the characteristics of each piece of equipment.

7. **Instruments:** List, and if appropirate describe, the instruments in this system.

8. **Safety and Emergency Procedures:** Provide details of safety regulations and emphasize special safety precautions that must be taken in the system. Tabulate hazards. Explain the type and location of safety equipment that is needed for this system.

9. **Appendices:** Check all available technical information to make sure that any relevant material that has not been included in the new manual is not lost. It should be included in appendices. These are most suited to information that is important but not regularly used in day-to-day operations, such as product details, temperatures, pressure tolerances, abbreviations, and calibration data.

Figure 7.4. Typical Page Formats for an Operator-Reference Manual

- **Standard Information Page** (ref. Figure 7.3, sections 2, 3, 5, 6, 7, 8) Most pages in a reference manual can be set out like this. This page layout is designed to be easily located and read. Each segment is treated as a separate document which can be updated easily, and for this reason pages are not numbered sequentially for the entire manual.

BOTANY WORKS	Section F178/F151		Document number 04-01
OLEFINES DIV	Subject OVERVIEW		
01	F178 storage vessel	This vessel provides storage for on-spec C_4 product from the debutaniser. The vessel's maximum capacity is 600 tons. The paired process relief safety valves have a set pressure of 440 kPAG. They discharge to the loading bay vent stack, and are interlocked to ensure one valve is always in service. They cannot discharge to the flari header, as little back pressure can be tolerated.	
		These valves blow to atmosphere. To avoid lifting any of them, a high pressure alarm is set at 389 kPag and a high pressure trip of the inlet value is set at 414 kPag.	
02	Normal operation	• Record once per shift the operating level of the C_4 sphere by reading the dip tape on top of the sphere. If the level exceeds 85%, the allowable ullage (94% liquid volume) will be exceeded and the high level alarm on the dip tape will trip shut the inlet EIV. C_4 product must then go to F151 or E8402 for vaporization into fuel-gas. Record tank pressure. Check for abnormalities. Check steam to tracing or level indicator impulse line.	
Date 20/8/92			Pg 1 of 5

- **Competency Guides** (ref. Figure 7.3, section 4) Each competency guide sets up step by step how to perform a task. This information is derived from a combination of task analysis and discussions with experienced operators.

BOTANY WORKS	Section F178/F151		Document number 09-13
OLEFINES DIV	Subject LOAD ROADTANKER FROM F178		
TASK		STEPS	KEY POINTS
01 Prepare tanker for loading		• MSA the tanker	
		• Driver to position the tanker into loading bay 3	
		• Place chocks under front and back wheels	Driver must switch off engine and apply handbrake
		• Connect earth strap to tanker	
		• Driver to connect liquid and vapor hose from truck to spout 5	
		• Driver to open liquid and vapor valves and vent the interspaces between tanker and spout isolation valves.	This step removes air in pumps
02 Check operation of J-173		• Open shand and jurs valve, and pump up to maximum pressure	
		• Check C_4 route through the filter (L-119)	A blocked filter would slow down or stop loading
		• Make sure that by-pass is shut	(Ref.12.4: Changing filters)
Date 20/8/92			Pg 1 of 2

simple diagrams, like the example shown in Figure 7.5, are adequate as long as they are clear.

4. *Proofread the guide and add any missing information.* Once the material is typed, check it carefully and correct any errors. There may be gaps or inconsistencies in the manual that become obvious by this stage and need to be fixed.

5. *Give the guide to a technical reviewer.* Before it can be finalized, the draft needs to be reviewed by one or two technical experts in the manual's subject matter. This validation process is very important, and those involved need to be made aware that errors that are allowed to slip through could have serious consequences.

Figure 7.5. Labeled Photos Are Useful in Technical Manuals

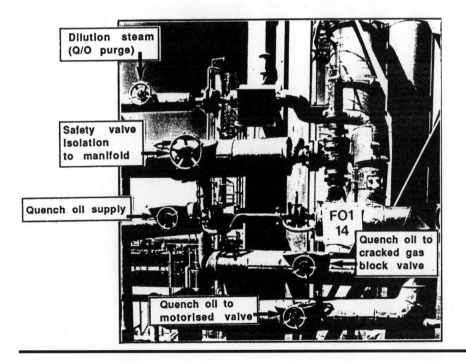

6. *Prepare the manual for printing.* During these last steps, final changes are made to the draft, and it is put together with diagrams and other graphic material so that it is ready for printing.

Organizing and Indexing Sections of the Manual

Many users of technical-reference manuals will be only occasional users who will need to find what they are looking for quickly. For this reason, each manual will need to have a simple, consistent system of indexing.

Here is one way of indexing a series of technical manuals. Each manual is given a unique two-digit code (01, 02,...99). Within each manual, each section is numbered sequentially (1, 2,...99), and again within each section, subjects are numbered sequentially (1, 2,...99). Figure 7.6 shows a set of manuals numbered in this way. Thus, the location code for "Overview of F178/F151" would be as follows:

$$27 - 2 - 2$$
manual — section — subject

Each section of the manual is treated as a separate document, and the pages in it are numbered sequentially starting with page one. This approach makes updating easier.

On-Line Job Aids

Although job-reference guides and technical-user manuals, are important aids, there are limits to their usefulness:

- Although it is possible to set reference guides or user manuals near the activity they deal with, for example, next to a counter or on a machine, they are not usually directly linked to doing the task.

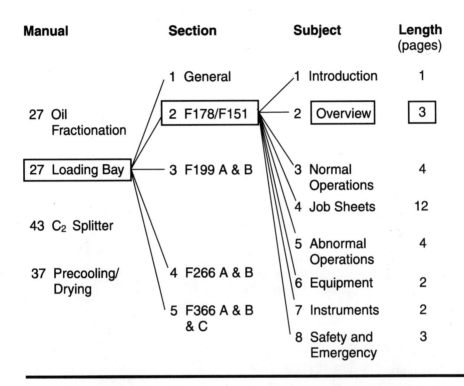

Figure 7.6. Section Numbering in a Series of Technical Manuals

- Employees with different skill levels need different aids. It is difficult to design a job aid that covers all the necessary steps and allows experienced employees to combine or skip certain steps or otherwise revise the steps as needed.

- Although job aids focus on the steps needed to complete a task, they do not explain why certain steps are needed. For example, a checklist might instruct a pilot to check that all systems are ready for take-off, but the job aid will not explain the reasons that certain parameters are set or what to do if something unusual happens.

Design and Use Job Aids

- In an organization in which there are multiple copies of manuals and there are regular changes to technology or procedures, the trainer will find it difficult to make sure that the manuals are kept up-to-date. Updating manuals by adding revised versions of documents can become a tedious and easily overlooked chore.

All of these factors have contributed to the greater use of on-line job aids. On-line job aids take three forms: help screens, procedural cues, and menus (Figure 7.7).

Figure 7.7. Different Types of On-Line Job Aids

Help Screens: Help screens advise system users what to do if they encounter problems —for example, if it is unclear what to do next or what information the system needs. In a typical computer system, the user simply presses a "help" key to divert to one or a series of "help" reference screens.

Procedural Cues: Some systems are designed to monitor operator behavior and to provide a prompt if something unusual is done. The prompt might be a warning message that the action attempted will lead to certain outcomes. The warning does not stop the operator from proceeding.

Menus: Most computer systems have built-in menus that let the operator skip to another part of the system to get information or modify incorrect variables.

Figure 7.8 shows why on-line job aids have gradually replaced job-reference guides and technical-user manuals in many jobs. Integration of the job aid with a computer system eliminates many of the problems that were discussed at the start of this section. In computer-based manufacturing, processing,

Figure 7.8. Examples of the Gradual Replacement of Paper Job Aids by On-Line Job Aids

	"Paper" Job Aids	On-Line Job Aids
Airline Industry	Pilots and other airline crew have regularly used standard lists for checking prior to take off and after landing.	Checking procedures are being incorporated with other functions into the pilots' integrated aircraft management system.
Banking Industry	A range of forms and job guides have been used to prompt bank workers to follow the required sequence and do calculations correctly.	Most bank transactions are now performed on a computer terminal. This prompts the teller to complete each step. Autotellers take this process one stage further and are designed to prompt customers to complete the transaction themselves.
Electronics Industry	Electronics technicians have made extensive use of manufacturers' reference manuals and other printed material to guide them in locating and rectifying faults.	Technicians are making greater use of portable computers for fault-finding and problem diagnosis. The technician can take the computer onto the site and connect it to the faulty equipment. The computer itself can run tests on the equipment and prompt the technician to take the necessary action via a display.

Design and Use Job Aids

and information systems, the on-line job aid is an integral part of performing the job. Such aids can have options that let both new and experienced employees get help as needed. On-line job aids can also be linked to detailed explanatory reference screens or to other media, like laser videodisc, to explain why as well as how something is done. Finally, on-line job aids are much easier to keep up-to-date than technical manuals, because they can be centrally revised.

As the examples presented in this section suggest, organizations will make more and more use of on-line job aids. These systems have the potential to significantly change the nature of the training needed.

End Notes

1. See A Handbook of Job Aids by Allison Rossett and Jeannette Gautier-Downes, 1991, San Diego, CA: Pfeiffer & Company.

2. Based in part on Cox and Stum (1985).

3. This format was adapted from suggestions in d'Agenais and Carruthers (1985) and was used by the author to design operator reference manuals for ICI's Olefines plant at Botany in Sydney, Australia. It is included here with the company's permission.

Bibliography

Beasley, B., & McLeod, J. (1983). *Guidelines for writing trade teaching materials.* Adelaide, Australia: National TAFE Centre for Research and Development.

Briggs, R. (1988, February). How will your operators react in an emergency? *Process Engineering.*

Cox, J., & Stum, S. (1985). The job aid. In H. Birnbrauer (Ed.), *The ASTD handbook for technical and skills training.* Alexandria, VA: American Society for Training and Development.

D'Agenais, J., & Carruthers, J. (1985). *Creating effective manuals.* Cincinnati, OH: South-Western Publishing.

Damodaran, L. (1981). The role of user support. In B. Schakel (Ed.), *Man-computer interaction: Human factors and aspects of computers and people*. Maryland: Sijthoff & Noordhoff.

Hartley, J. (1978). *Designing instructional text*. London: Kogan Page.

Kearsley, G. (1984). *Training and technology*. Reading, MA: Addison-Wesley.

Riley, S. (1986). User understanding. In D. Norman and S. Draper (Eds.), *User-centred system design*. Hillsdale, NJ: Lawrence Erlbaum.

Now if you'll just describe the process one step at a time, and I'll write it down. . .

Structure a Training Program

In order to plan a training program, the trainer will need to make many decisions about the program's structure. Chapter 8 looks at some of the factors that influence the sequence and structure of individual training sessions and training programs.

Decisions about structure are necessary at three different levels (Figure 8.1):

At the narrowest level, where the trainer is concerned with the parts of an individual training session, he or she often has to plan instruction with a view toward encouraging learners to behave in particular ways. For example, an operator may have to learn to take certain actions if a warning signal appears on a screen. The structure of each part of a training session can help to develop this and other types of responses.

At a broader level, where the focus is on one or more training sessions, the trainer may need to plan a training sequence that incorporates explanations, demonstrations, and practice. These three elements need to be integrated if they are to be used to good effect.

Finally, at the broadest level, where the aim is to develop training for a whole organization or industry, some of the issues that need to be considered are as follows on the next page:

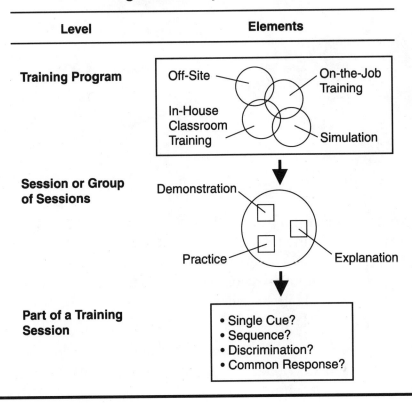

Figure 8.1. Decisions About Structure at the Three Program-Development Levels

- ♦ How trainers can use competency profiles to structure training;

- ♦ How to train employees to operate complex integrated technologies; and

- ♦ What the main options are for providing skills training.

Chapter 8 looks at each of the three levels in turn and discusses some of the factors that influence a trainer's decisions about structure at each level. The chapter then makes the point that no matter how well a training program is structured, the skills that are learned need to be applied on the job. Chapter 8 ends with a number of suggestions for ensuring that this transfer of learning occurs.

The Structure of Skills Training

The way that the parts of a training session are structured depends on the type of response that is being handled. One way of classifying the responses that learners have to acquire is shown in Figure 8.2. These responses are arranged in a more or less hierarchical manner, from the most specific and discrete to the most general and interrelated.

The following section looks at each type of response and briefly examines some training strategies that are appropriate for each response.

Figure 8.2. Types of Learner Responses

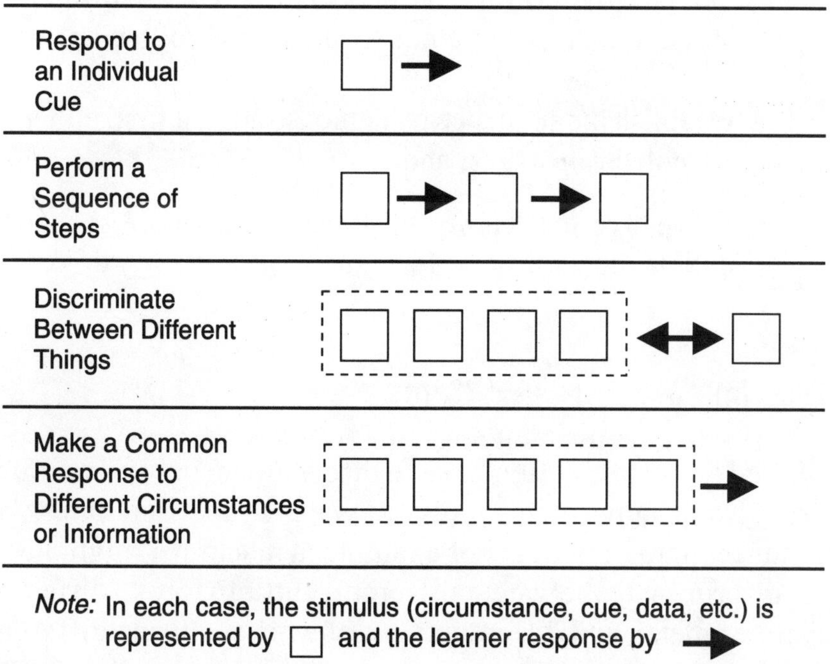

Respond to an Individual Cue	□→
Perform a Sequence of Steps	□→□→□
Discriminate Between Different Things	┌─────────────┐ │ □ □ □ □ │ ↔ □ └─────────────┘
Make a Common Response to Different Circumstances or Information	┌─────────────┐ │ □ □ □ □ □ │→ └─────────────┘

Note: In each case, the stimulus (circumstance, cue, data, etc.) is represented by □ and the learner response by →

Structure a Training Program ♦ **127**

Respond to an Individual Cue

If a learner is required to respond to warning lights on a control panel or to a symbol on a screen, the trainer can support the desired responses to individual cues like these by doing the following:

- Presenting the cue and then guiding the learner through the steps to make the desired response;
- Reinforcing the desired response (for example, commenting on it in an encouraging way); and
- Scheduling regular practice.

Perform a Sequence of Steps

If a learner has to follow a fixed sequence of steps to dismantle a piece of equipment, the trainer should do the following:

- Establish the sequence by demonstrating it first, either as a whole or in stages; and
- Encourage the learner to practice the whole sequence until he or she can perform the sequence smoothly.

Discriminate Between Items

Skilled employees often have to discriminate between different system conditions, tools, raw materials, outcomes, or product characteristics. For example, a machinist might need to discriminate between different cutting tools, different types of metal, and different types of work requiring different approaches. Trainers can help employees to discriminate by doing the following:

- Initially making the differences between the items as noticeable as possible;
- Presenting the whole set of items at the same time;
- Encouraging learners to think about the differences and to discriminate for themselves;
- Moving from obvious differences to more subtle ones;
- Initially removing any factors likely to be distracting from the discrimination task; and
- Gradually introducing more actual workplace factors into the discrimination task and helping learners learn not to be sidetracked by them.

Respond to Different Circumstances or Information

Suppose that an operator has to learn that when conditions X, Y, and Z occur, a system is malfunctioning and he or she needs to shut down a production line. In this case, the trainer needs to teach the operator to make a particular response to factors. The trainer can achieve this goal by doing the following:

- Presenting all the conditions (X, Y, and Z) at the same time so that the employee can start to recognize that these conditions have the same implications or consequences;
- Guiding the employee to make the desired response, such as "shut down the line," to the different conditions; and
- Encouraging the employee to distinguish between the relevant conditions (X, Y, and Z) and other conditions that might appear similar.

Combining Explanations, Demonstrations, and Practice

Suppose that some employees have to be trained to perform a task consisting of ten steps. The trainer will probably want to explain the overall task and how each step is done, demonstrate the sequence, and provide an opportunity for practice. But what is the best way to structure the session or module so that these three elements—explanation, demonstration, and practice—are used to their best advantage?

There are a variety of effective ways to structure this type of training. Some of the options you might consider are as follows:

- Covering the whole task or only a part of the task;
- Following the actual sequence or a modified sequence; or
- Using continuous or interspersed practice.

This section looks at each of these options and examines the conditions that indicate which of the choices are appropriate in each case.

The Whole Task or Part of the Task

The whole or just a part of a task can be covered in a single training session (Figure 8.3). The trainer should cover the whole task in a single session when the following statements are true:

- The relationship between the stages of a task need to be shown;
- The subject matter consists of a meaningful whole;
- The skills needed to perform each part of a task are similar; and

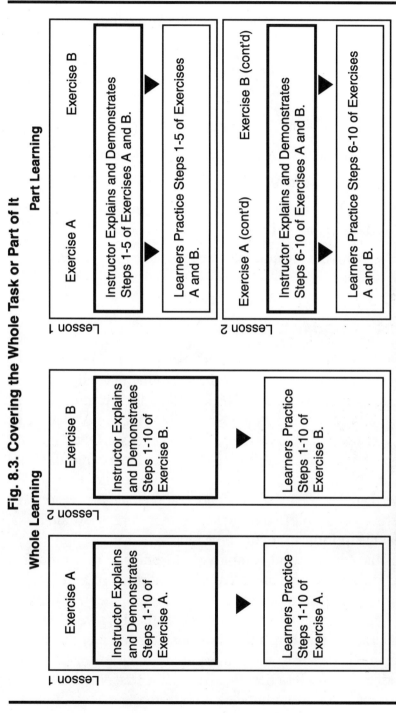

Fig. 8.3. Covering the Whole Task or Part of It

Note: This diagram assumes that learners are required to complete two exercises over two training sessions. To simplify the diagram, it is assumed that each exercise consists of ten steps.

Structure a Training Program ♦ **131**

* Employees are experienced and can relate the new task to what they already know.

Divide the task into parts when the following statements are true:

* The task is long and complex;
* The difficulty levels of the steps vary considerably;
* The subject matter is not part of a meaningful whole;
* Time limitations preclude covering the whole activity in one session; and
* Employees are new and need to learn slowly over several sessions.

Actual or Modified Sequence

In planning demonstrations and practice periods, the trainer will not always need to go through the steps that make up a task in the natural order (Figure 8.4). For example, the trainer might change the order and demonstrate the tasks and then have employees practice the last steps first. The reason that this could be appropriate is that once employees have mastered the final steps in a sequence, they are more likely to understand the eventual goal of the procedure and to appreciate the reasons for earlier steps. A modified sequence is, therefore, useful in training people to follow lengthy procedures.

If the trainer wants employees to practice in a modified sequence, the trainer may have to do more work beforehand, preparing things like samples, pieces of equipment, and materials. For example, in a competency area that involves selection of materials, setting up machines, making some components, and assembling them, the trainer might have to make up the components himself or herself so that in the first practice session employees can start with the assembly steps.

Continuous or Interspersed Practice

Practice sessions can either consist of a continuous segment, or they can be divided into shorter intervals interspersed with explanations and demonstrations (Figure 8.5). Interspersed practice, the second approach, is said to be "spaced." In general, spaced practice is superior to continuous practice for both learning and recall. For this reason, try to do the following:

- ♦ Avoid lengthy workshop practice sessions;
- ♦ Vary the pace of practical instruction so that practice is available between short demonstrations and other activities; and

Figure 8.4. Following the Actual Sequence or a Modified Sequence

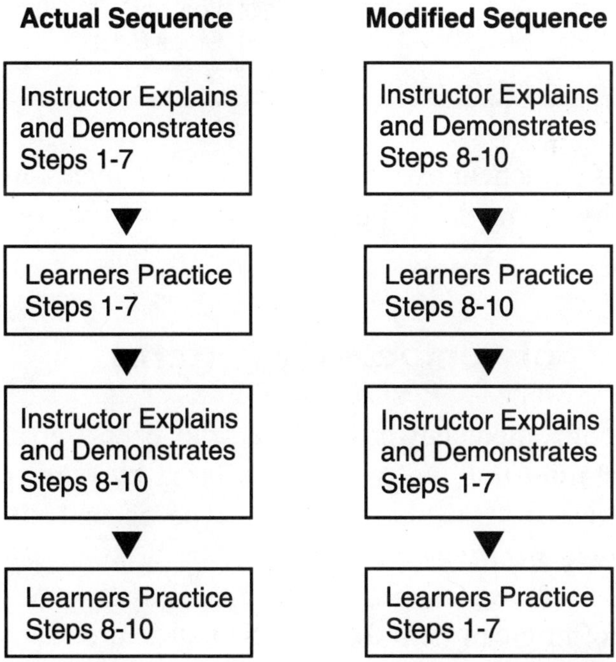

Actual Sequence	Modified Sequence
Instructor Explains and Demonstrates Steps 1-7	Instructor Explains and Demonstrates Steps 8-10
▼	▼
Learners Practice Steps 1-7	Learners Practice Steps 8-10
▼	▼
Instructor Explains and Demonstrates Steps 8-10	Instructor Explains and Demonstrates Steps 1-7
▼	▼
Learners Practice Steps 8-10	Learners Practice Steps 1-7

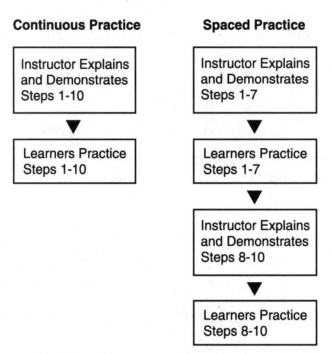

Figure 8.5. Examples of Continuous Practice or Spaced Practice

- Use practical exercises that give employees an opportunity to practice skills they have learned previously.

Analysis of Competency Patterns

Analysis of competency patterns has often been used as the basis for structuring training programs offered by other providers, such as industry skill centers. This type of analysis is called *competency profiling*.

The following simplified example illustrates how competency profiling can help to determine structure. Suppose that, within an industry, there are three categories of employees

Figure 8.6. The Use of Competency Profiling to Plan Modular Training

The competency profiles for workers of types A, B, and C in an industry are shown below:

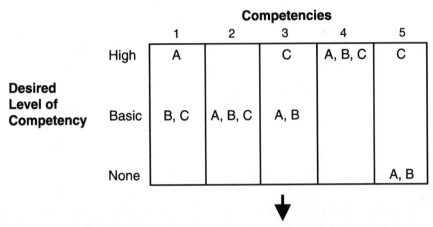

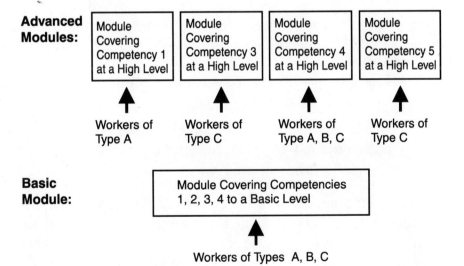

Structure a Training Program ♦ **135**

(types A, B, and C) whose jobs can be described in terms of only five competencies. The top half of Figure 8.6 shows the competency levels needed by each of the three types of employees. In real studies of this sort, statistical techniques such as cluster analysis are used to separate competencies into groups. Despite its artificial simplicity, however, our example illustrates the basic principles.

Information about competency patterns can be very helpful in structuring training programs. The bottom half of Figure 8.6 illustrates a program structure that corresponds to the competency groupings shown. It consists of a basic training module covering competencies 1 to 4, supplemented by advanced modules dealing with competencies 1, 3, 4, and 5 for those who need them.

This example also illustrates another important point about competency profiles and program structure. If no distinction had been made here between the three types of employees, that is, if all the competency data had been combined, then the desired level of competency in each case would have appeared to be somewhere in the middle between "high" and "none," which would be wrong. The following result would have occurred:

- Employees who needed advanced training would not have received it; and
- Employees in categories A and B would probably have been required to have competency 5 training, even though they did not need it.

For these reasons trainers need to take occupational subcategories into account when structuring a training program. Once it is clear which target groups have to be trained, the trainer can develop an appropriate program structure that suits each group.

Training Employees to Operate Complex Integrating Technologies

A number of the more advanced manufacturing and data-management systems that are introduced into industries are imported. Often the training that accompanies the introduction of these systems is provided as an afterthought. To keep this from happening, trainers should try to maintain an ongoing involvement with what is happening in the organization so that they can contribute to discussions about future directions, goals, and strategies. If possible, the trainer should work alongside technical personnel during the design, planning, installation, and phasing in of new equipment and systems. Training plans also need to take into account the fact that, at least until new technologies are fully operational, no one on site will have complete mastery.

Training should begin well before systems are installed and should start with the most skilled employees. This allows them to be involved in installation, to begin to use the equipment, and to train others. It also maximizes the ownership of new technology and minimizes the insecurity caused by its introduction.

In order for employees to learn to operate such a system effectively, they need to develop a mental picture of the system. Although this type of learning is not fully understood, research to date suggests that training programs can encourage the development of systems thinking by doing the following:

- Building up operator knowledge of the system in stages (Figure 8.7, Strategy 1), rather than providing a superficial overview and then attempting to build on that (Strategy 2). The best strategy is to start with the most general and simple model of the system and, through a mixture of discovery learning and formal instruction, to introduce more and more functions and components;

Figure 8.7. Instructional Strategies for Training on Complex Integrated Technologies

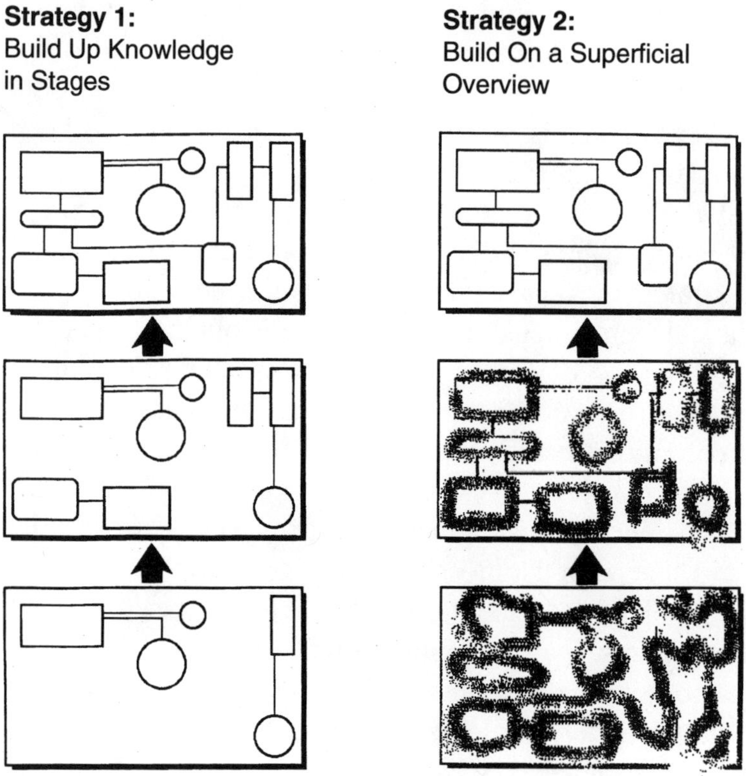

Strategy 1:
Build Up Knowledge in Stages

Strategy 2:
Build On a Superficial Overview

- Showing employees how new integrated systems are related to, and have developed from, equipment and processes with which they are familiar; and

- Encouraging employees to build up their own personalized schematic diagrams of the system and then to test them out. Testing can be achieved by making predictions that can be evaluated in exercises involving system adjustment and use.

General Approaches to Skills Training

This section describes four general approaches to skills training and analyzes the merits of each (Figure 8.8). The four approaches are as follows:

- Off-site training
- In-house training
- Computer simulation
- On-the-job training

Off-Site Training

A great deal of training takes place away from the workplace. There are many training providers, such as industry-wide skills centers, private training schools, materials suppliers, universities, equipment manufacturers, and other agencies.

Off-site training by external providers has a number of advantages:

- An effective instructional environment is more easily provided for the employees;

Figure 8.8. Four Broad Approaches to Training

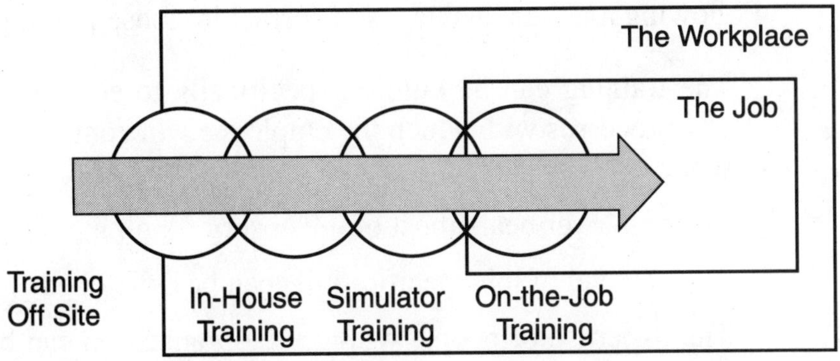

- Instructors are likely to be highly skilled;
- Employees are more likely to receive a sound conceptual understanding of the job; and
- Employees are likely to receive recognized certificates after they have completed the training program.

The disadvantages of this approach are as follows:

- Simulating complex technical systems may be difficult;
- The training provided may not be related closely enough to the job; and
- Large organizations are often slow to respond to changing needs and may not send their employees for training.

Formal In-House Training

Training can be provided in-house in a number of ways, including technician schools and in-house training programs. The term *formal training* as used here means training that is structured and takes place away from the job.

Formal in-house training covers the whole gamut of training areas: machine operators, trainees, those preparing to operate new equipment, and personnel being retrained to meet changing skill requirements.

Following are the advantages of formal in-house training:

- The training can be tailored specifically to equipment and processes with which the employee will continue to work;
- The employer bears most of the cost of training;
- A high level of job-specific skills can be developed;
- The expertise of people within the organization can be used easily; and

- More attention can be paid to the link between classroom training and subsequent work.

Following are the disadvantages of this approach:

- The training may not be cost effective if there are not many learners;
- Batch training of new workers may be encouraged, which means that people starting work on different dates may have to wait for training to be offered; and
- Some complex technical systems are hard to cover in formal in-house training.

Computer Simulation

Computer simulation refers to the use of a computer to produce models of activities, processes, or equipment, for example, an operator console or an aircraft cockpit. Computer simulation can be part of a total work environment or vestibule training, such as a bank branch or a production line. Simulation and computer-based training are covered in detail in Chapter 10.

Following are the advantages of computer simulation:

- The training is interactive;
- The weaknesses of individual employees are targeted;
- The order of instruction optimizes learning;
- Disruption to production is avoided; and
- Learning takes place away from normal work pressures.

Following are the disadvantages of this approach:

- Establishing the training is expensive;

- Keeping simulators up-to-date may be difficult; and
- A balance in the number of learners may be difficult to achieve. (If there are too few learners, the facility may not be cost effective. If there are too many, the training may not be very effective.)

On-the-Job Training

On-the-job training refers to all the types of training that occur at the workplace under the guidance of an experienced employee, a supervisor, or a trainer. It is discussed in detail in Chapter 9. On-the-job training can be done in a fairly formal, planned way, or it can simply be a matter of an experienced employee's keeping an eye on the learner and answering questions and correcting mistakes.

Following are the advantages of on-the-job training:

- Learners are assured employment once they are trained;
- Different learning rates can be accommodated;
- The relationship between the learner and the trainer is usually supportive;
- No special training equipment is needed;
- The skills learned are directly linked to the workplace and can be practiced immediately; and
- The learner is productive and, therefore, able to contribute to the cost of training.

Following are the disadvantages of this approach:

- The ratio of one occasional trainer to one or two learners may not be cost effective;
- Errors made during training can cause problems, because training occurs in the workplace;

- There may be conflict over the need for output (products or services), the maintenance of technical systems, and on-the-job training; and

- Some tasks might be better learned in a modified sequence.

Transfer of Skills to the Job

No matter how well a training program is structured, it will not be effective if the competencies that are acquired are not applied on the job. Research into this area suggests that to maximize the likelihood that what an employee learns continues to be practiced and used at the workplace, the trainer should try to do the following:

- Make sure that employees have mastered competencies before the training program ends;

- Incorporate opportunities in the program for employees to plan how they intend to apply what they have learned;

- Build employees' confidence;

- Minimize the time between training and the opportunity for workplace practice.

Even if the trainer does these things, the job environment itself can still prevent skills from being transferred from a formal training program to the workplace. Aspects of the job environment likely to hinder the transfer of competencies to the workplace include the following:

- Inappropriate or faulty equipment;

- Work pressures;

- Conflicting or unclear job descriptions;
- Inadequate financial and interpersonal rewards; and
- An organizational culture that is depressed, fragmented, or conflict-ridden.

Although some of these factors may be outside the trainer's control, others can and should be modified.

Bibliography

Annett, J., & Sparrow, J. (1985). Transfer of training: A review of research and practical implications. *PLET, 22*(2).

Brown, J., & Newman, S. (1985). Issues in cognitive and social ergonomics: From our house to bauhaus. *Human-Computer Interaction,* pp. 359-391.

Davies, I. (1973). *Competency-based learning: Technology, management and design.* New York: McGraw-Hill.

Dobler, G. (1986). Technical education for a successful implementation of CAD systems. In H. Bullinger (Ed.), *Human factors in manufacturing.* (4th IAO Conference Proceedings, Stuttgart, 1985). Bedford, UK: IFS Publications.

Fox, R. (1984). Fostering transfer of learning to work environments. In T. Sork (Ed.), *Designing and implementing effective workshops* (New Directions for Continuing Education, No. 22). San Francisco, CA: Jossey-Bass.

Miller, V. (1979). *International guidebook for trainers in business and industry.* New York: Van Nostrand Reinhold.

Sinclair, M. (1988). Future AMT and ergonomics: Knowledge, organizational issues and human roles. *Applied Ergonomics, 19*(1).

Stammers, R., & Patrick, J. (1975). *The psychology of training.* London: Methuen.

Whiting, J. (1988). New perspectives on open and distance learning for adult audiences. In D. Harris (Ed.), *Education for new technologies.* London: Kogan Page.

On-the-job training is an efficient economical way to train employees

Train On-the-Job

The term *on-the-job training* (OJT) refers to training that is done at the workplace by an experienced employee, a supervisor, or a trainer. The process itself is fairly straightforward. The experienced employee or whoever else is doing the training usually begins by explaining and then demonstrating the competency, while the learner watches and listens. The learner then attempts the competency under the trainer's guidance. The trainer gives the learner feedback, and the learner continues to practice under supervision until he or she attains a satisfactory standard. At that point, the learner might move on to the next competency.

On-the-job training varies considerably in terms of formality and degree of structure. It can be planned very carefully using session objectives, a step-by-step plan, and training aids, or it might simply involve an experienced employee's demonstrating a competency for a learner and then occasionally following up with the learner to see if he or she has any questions or needs help.

On-the-job training is an efficient, economical way of providing training that is immediately applicable. Not much is written about it, yet more skill learning probably takes place on the job than anywhere else. On-the-job training is particularly suited to training in medium- to small-sized organizations.

Some countries ascribe to the importance of on-the-job training more than others. The Japanese, for example, believe that to learn new skills, learners have to work alongside more experienced employees. Guidance is provided by supervisors, but learner self-direction is emphasized. The expectation is that learners will ask for help when they need it.

This idea that employees have a lot of the responsibility for learning is important. On-the-job training could be assumed to mean an instructional approach in which skills are transferred from an experienced employee to an unskilled and passive learner. But a view like this ignores the active nature of learning. Remember the example of learners as navigators that was discussed in Chapter 3? That example pointed out that most people do not want to sit back and be guided through learning something new. They would prefer to try to learn themselves, using outside help when needed. The process described in this chapter might be more accurately called *on-the-job learning*.

Chapter 9 deals with on-the-job training and learning. It describes the phases that a skilled employee or a supervisor might go through to train someone. The chapter then discusses the broader issue of workplace learning and suggests ways in which the work site can become a place where learning and skill development are encouraged.

Conducting On-the-Job Training

If a trainer has to conduct on-the-job training to teach someone how to perform a task, the trainer's approach could vary. His or her approach will depend on factors such as the nature of the task, the employee's previous experience, the amount of preparation time the trainer has, and the organization's culture. However, there are some things that are usually important no matter what approach is taken. These can be grouped into five overlapping phases:

- Planning the training;
- Making contact with the learner;
- Demonstrating the task;
- Supervising practice; and
- Linking the training to the workplace.

The main considerations during each of these phases are discussed in the remainder of this section.

Planning the Training

The trainer will need to do several things during the planning phase:

Break the task into manageable pieces. If the trainer tries to cover too much information in a single training session, the learner may not understand the information. The trainer needs to divide the task into segments and to check that the learner understands each segment. The learner's understanding can be checked by asking him or her to answer questions or to perform the task.

Write a session outline. This can be written in the same format used to prepare a demonstration lesson (see Chapter 12 for details). The session outline could also be a piece of paper that lists the main points or steps that will be covered. Competency guides, which were discussed in Chapter 4, can also be used as session outlines.

Decide on the sequence of the training. There are many factors that affect the sequence of the training (see Chapter 8 for details). The trainer should use the following guidelines:

- Start by showing the purpose of the training, for example, a finished product;

- First explain the simple skills and then explain the more complex skills;

- Start from what the learner can already do and then move on to new skills; and

- Follow the routine sequence of steps as far as possible.

Make sure that the trainer can do the task. If the trainer is not familiar with the competency area, he or she may need to review it in order to be able to demonstrate it in a clear, logical way;

Decide what time to start and what time to end the training session. Starting and finishing times depend on such conditions as the difficulty of the task, the time it takes to perform it, and the learner's attention span. Try to avoid interruptions caused by lunch breaks, other employees, quitting time, equipment unavailability, and phone calls.

Make Contact with the Learner

When the training begins, try to make contact with the learner. The trainer will be physically alongside the learner, but that is not the same as actually engaging with the learner so that the two understand each other. A friendly, open approach that encourages conversation is important in order to make contact. The learner is more likely to take in what the trainer is offering if the trainer respects him or her and treats the learner as an adult.

Training should build on what learners already know and can do. To find that out, the trainer should ask the learner when they first meet where he or she has worked and what competencies he or she has mastered. At the same time, the trainer should try to find out if the learner has had any difficulties in learning.

While establishing contact, the trainer should give the learner an overview of what is to be covered and explain how it relates to the rest of the job. Where the trainer positions himself or herself will also affect the rapport he or she has with the learner. While talking and getting ready to start training, the trainer should position himself or herself to be able to reach all the equipment needed and to be alongside—and not opposite—the learner. The learner should be in his or her usual work area. For example, if the trainer is demonstrating how to operate a data terminal, the learner should be seated in front of his or her data terminal, and the trainer should sit beside the learner.

Demonstrate the Task

A straightforward way of demonstrating a task is to go through the procedure once at normal speed and then do it again slowly. While demonstrating the task, the trainer should explain each step to the learner; show the learner what tools are needed, which adjustments need to be made, and why each step is important. After every few steps, the trainer should ask the learner questions to make sure the learner has followed the procedure. Attention should be drawn to any aspects of the procedure that are dangerous or particularly difficult.

There are many variations on this approach. These are covered in detail in Chapters 8 and 12. Some of the main aspects of giving a demonstration as part of on-the-job training are as follows:

Emphasize safety and quality. When conducting on-the-job training, the trainer communicates with much more than just the words. The emphasis that the trainer gives to certain points and his or her facial expressions and hand gestures all contribute to the message that is conveyed. The trainer should think about these aspects of communication. On-the-job training is not concerned only with doing routine tasks but also with other important aspects of the job, such as working safely and at a high standard. The trainer's attitude and method of communicating, both verbally and nonverbally, can encourage the learner's development of the skills necessary for safe work practices and high-quality work.

Show the big picture first. The trainer should start the training session by showing the learner how the task fits into the job as a whole. Although this may be obvious to the trainer, he or she should not assume that the same is true for the learner.

The trainer may find that it is easier to understand the need to provide context if he or she thinks about what is involved in explaining to some travelers how to get to a particular place (Figure 9.1). If the trainer does not say anything about the surrounding area (Map a), the travelers probably will not have any idea about where their destination fits in. If the trainer includes all the surrounding towns and landmarks (Map b), they may become overwhelmed. The trainer's aim should be to include just enough detail (Map c) so that the travelers can reach their destination.

Similarly, during on-the-job training, the trainer needs to provide just enough detail about the context of the task. The trainer might say briefly what the task's purpose is, why it has to be done in a particular way (in terms of the overall job), and how it links to other tasks. In addition, the trainer should explain the meaning of any technical terms or jargon words that are crucial to the task but leave out less important terms and information until the learner has started to become familiar with the task.

Plan for and encourage active learning. The trainer needs to take into account the active nature of learning. Most people are keen to learn new skills and will try their best to link what they are shown to what they already know. This natural inclination to learn should be supported. The trainer can support the inclination to learn by doing the following:

- Encouraging learners to work together in groups to share experiences and to help one another;

Figure 9.1. Providing the Right Amount of Information About Context

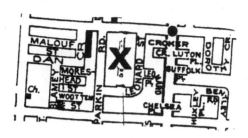

Map a: Too little contextual information.

Map b: Too much contextual information.

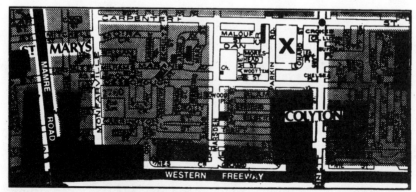

Map c: Adequate contextual information.

Train On-the-Job ♦ **153**

- Explaining what the task involves and why it is important;
- Reinforcing each learner's progress by commenting on it;
- Being supportive and understanding when mistakes are made;
- Recognizing that each learner has a range of experiences and competencies that can be built on;
- Showing the learners that the trainer is there to support their skill development, rather than to train them to follow a routine; and
- Using metaphors, visual images, and tangible examples to explain abstract concepts or processes that cannot be observed.

Avoid criticizing learners. On-the-job training is difficult to perform well, and many supervisors or workers who occasionally train others feel insecure in the role. The trainer will find that projecting his or her feelings of inadequacy onto the learner is easy. In other words, the trainer can mask his or her own insecurity by directing critical comments at the learner. Comments such as the following should be avoided:

> I'm amazed it took you so long to do it. One of my kids could have done it faster than that.

> I don't know what they teach these days at schools. We used to all learn how to do that right at the start.

The trainer should not make comments like these, because they can seriously undermine the effectiveness of training. Instead, the trainer should learn how to cope with his or her own insecurities rather than project these insecurities onto others. The trainer should remember how he or she felt when learning to do something new and should think about what comments were most helpful.

Supervise Practice

The learner will need to practice doing the task under the trainer's supervision. The following would be a good motto for on-the-job training:

> I hear and I forget
> I see and I remember
> I do and I understand
> —*Adapted from Confucius*

As soon as the learner has grasped the fundamentals of the task, the trainer should encourage him or her to practice while the trainer observes. The trainer should answer any questions during this process and check the learner's understanding by having him or her explain the main steps and how they fit into the task as a whole. Practice under supervision is particularly important, because the trainer can immediately correct any mistakes the learner makes and ensure that the learner is taught the correct approach. If work groups are acceptable in the learner's work environment, he or she should be encouraged to practice in a work group so that the group members can support one another's skill development.

Link Training to the Workplace

The last phase of on-the-job training involves making sure that the learner continues to develop the skills he or she learned. This is mainly a matter of practice and ongoing support. The learner is more likely to build on what he or she has been taught if the trainer does the items listed on the following page:

- Continues to oversee the learner's work until he or she has mastered the task;
- Talks with the learner about different ways to apply the same routine procedure in different circumstances;
- Leaves the learner feeling confident that he or she is a worthwhile person and has the potential to become more skilled;
- Encourages the learner to take pride in his or her work;
- Makes sure that there is some ongoing opportunity for the learner to practice; and
- Makes it clear who the learner should go to for help if difficulties arise.

The trainer should remember that getting learners to continue to apply and build on what they have learned is more than a simple educational challenge. The learners' failure to transfer what they have learned in training to their job environment can be related to a range of factors, including these:

- The efficiency of workplace technology;
- Built-in rewards for taking shortcuts in relation to safety;
- Excessive work pressures;
- A poor work environment;
- Inadequate supervision;
- Too much conflict in the organization;
- Insufficient rewards for skill development;
- Conflicting job descriptions; and
- The absence of a feedback mechanism that draws attention to errors.

If the training that is provided fails to produce results, the trainer may need to investigate broader problems such as these.

Encouraging Learning at the Workplace

So far, this chapter has concentrated on ways of conducting on-the-job training. This is important, but for on-the-job training to be effective, the organization needs to support learning. There are a number of ways in which trainers can encourage learning at the workplace and can contribute to the development of an organizational culture that supports learning. Some of these methods are as follows:

- Make it clear that the trainer's role is concerned not only with classroom training, but also with the whole process of skill formation.

- Follow up with learners after they have completed classroom training, and try to make sure that they can practice and build on what they have learned.

- Introduce ways for employees to learn at the time, place, and pace that matches their individual needs. In recent years, the United Kingdom, for example, has experimented widely with "open-learning" approaches to training and development.

- Establish a network of people responsible for learning at all levels. Figure 9.2 shows how this might operate in a organization with different organizational levels.

    - The network in this approach consists of the following:
    - A training manager who administers the training program and provides advice on learning approaches, needs analysis, skills assessment, and similar issues;

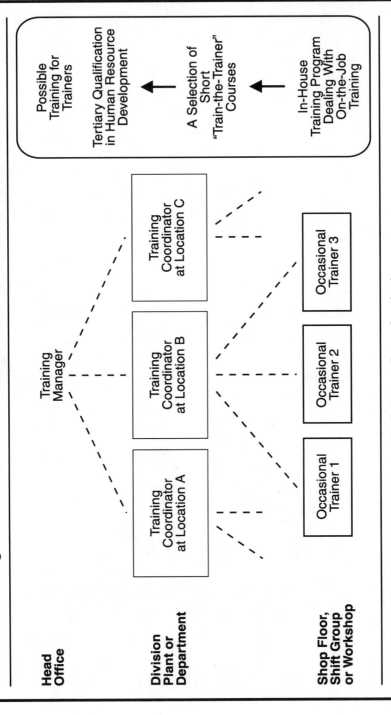

Fig. 9.2. A Network of Trainers at Different Organizational Levels

- Full-time trainers for each division, plant, or department who conduct formal training, maintain competency-assessment records, develop instructional resources, and facilitate workplace learning; and
- Occasional trainers who are workers or supervisors who do some on-the-job training and some formal classroom training but who also support workplace learning as part of their day-to-day work.

• Provide whiteboards and other appropriate instructional aids adjacent to work areas and encourage occasional trainers to use them.

• Focus your efforts on activities that are realistic and related to workplace conditions and to what employees feel they need.

• Promote discovery learning. This can be done by providing opportunities for learners to think about work problems, to investigate what happens in particular situations, to formulate hypotheses and to test them out, and to take responsibility for applying their conclusions. Discovery learning needs to be introduced carefully to avoid safety hazards, damage to equipment, or the anger that might result from learners' feeling that they are not adequately supported.

• Provide training for employees and supervisors who are required to do some occasional training and encourage them to adopt a learner-centered approach.

• Provide basic job aids, such as reference manuals, charts, and help screens for computer systems.

• Recognize the inevitability of trainers' having different priorities from those of production managers and maintenance staff. For example, production deadlines can often make it difficult for supervisors to leave time for workplace learning. These conflicts of interest need to be aired openly on an ongoing basis so that compromises can be reached that still leave scope for skill development.

The general goal of trainers should be to change working places into learning places, that is, places where workers, supervisors, and managers are able to upgrade their skills and knowledge as a normal part of their working lives and where, through the processes of consultation and training, everyone is encouraged to be effective in the dual roles of learner and helper of learning.

Bibliography

Boud, D. (Ed.). (1988). *Developing student autonomy in learning.* London: Kogan Page.

Charner, I., & Rolzinski, A. (1987, Spring). *Responding to the educational needs of today's workplace* (Higher Education Sourcebook Series No. 33, Chapters 8 & 9). San Francisco, CA: Jossey-Bass.

Feuer, D. (1986, July). Growing your own technical experts. *Training,* pp. 23-26.

Fox, R. (1984). Fostering transfer of learning to work environments. In T. Sork (Ed.), *Designing and implementing effective workshops.* San Francisco, CA: Jossey-Bass.

Garratt, B. (1987). *The learning organization.* London: Fontana.

Hewitt, C. (1988). Education in new technologies for those in employment. In D. Harris (Ed.), *Education for the new technologies.* London: Kogan Page.

Koike, K. (1983). The formation of worker skill in small Japanese firms. *Japanese Economics Studies, 11*(4).

Magnum, S. (1985, February). On-the-job vs classroom training: Some deciding factors. *Training,* pp. 75-77.

Marsick, V. (1987). *Learning in the workplace.* London: Croom Helm.

Marsick, V. (1988). Learning in the workplace: the case for reflectivity and critical reflectivity. *Adult Education Quarterly, 38*(4).

Rehder, R. (1983, January). Education and training: Have the Japanese beaten us again. *Personnel Journal.*

Schon, D. (1987). *Educating the reflective practitioner.* San Francisco, CA: Jossey-Bass.

In the past few years, technology has affected every aspect of work

Use Computers in Training

Rapid technological change combined with a shortage of skilled workers in organizations have led to strenuous attempts to find quicker and more cost-effective approaches to training. A number of organizations have looked to computer-based training as an important part of their training strategy.

In computer-based training, the learning program is contained in the computer, and the learner interacts with this program via the keyboard or some other input device such as a handheld "mouse" or a touchscreen. Diagrams, tables of information, video sequences, text, and questions can all appear on the computer screen.

Computer-based training is becoming more widely used for skills training. There are a number of reasons for this:

- Input devices such as the touchscreen and mouse, as well as software developments such as the pull-down menu, have all made computers easier to use.

- The cost of the equipment (hardware) and the programs (software) has decreased as microcomputers have become widely available.

- The development of better programs has made it easier for trainers to write computer-based training programs without expert help or programming knowledge.

- The increase of personal computers at work and home has made people more receptive to using them in training programs.

- The development of laser-videodisc technology, which allows rapid access to any part of a video sequence, has made it easier to link text with high-quality moving images.

- The increased impact of computers on skilled work has made it easier to integrate training with day-to-day operations. For example, retail stock control, travel bookings, and manufacturing processes are all normally computer controlled.

These trends are sure to continue, and trainers are likely to use computers increasingly for skills training.

Chapter 10 provides an overview of computer-based training. It examines the terminology and shows how computers and laser videodisc can be used to provide instruction and to manage training. The chapter outlines the factors that need to be considered in deciding whether computer-based training is appropriate and provides guidelines on how to overcome resistance to computer-based training.

Computers in Training

The terminology used in computer training needs to be explained before the various ways in which computers can be used in skills training can be discussed. There are a number of terms used to describe the use of computers in training, and these terms have caused some confusion. In fact, any combination of the three columns of words listed in Figure 10.1 can be created.

Many of the resulting combinations have similar or even identical meanings. Although there is no general agreement on terminology, the phrase *computer-based training* is probably the term that is most commonly used to describe any activity that relies on computers to support training. This is the term that is used throughout this book. Computer-based training (CBT) covers two different, although closely linked, areas: computer-aided learning (CAL) and computer-managed learning (CML). The relationship between these terms is shown schematically in Figure 10.2.

In computer-aided learning, whatever is to be learned is contained in the computer program, and the learners use the program for instruction. In contrast, computer-managed learning refers to the use of a computer program to keep track of a learner's progress. The following paragraphs highlight this distinction and illustrate the range of computer-based training programs available.

Figure 10.1. Terms Used to Describe Computers as a Training Medium

Computer	X	Aided Assisted Based Enhanced Managed Supported	X	Education Learning Instruction Teaching Training

Figure 10.2. Computer-Aided Learning and Computer-Based Training

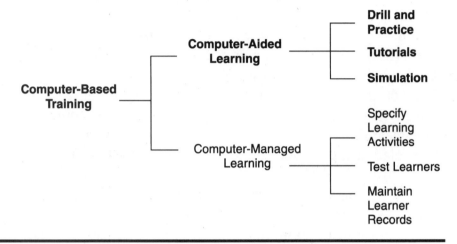

Computer-Aided Learning

There are many ways in which computers can be used to aid learning. For example, there is a wide range of software available, from simple off-the-shelf programs to sophisticated programs that can be individually tailored to meet the needs of a particular organization. Similarly, there are a number of different types of computer equipment and these can be applied to different aspects of training. Software and hardware can also be combined in a variety of ways.

In recent years, computer-aided learning programs have been used to train the following:

- Bank tellers to complete customer transactions;
- Air-traffic controllers to monitor a sector of air space;
- Credit-union personnel to guide customers through a loan-application form;
- Technicians to diagnose and rectify problems;

- Mail-sorting staff to quickly and accurately type destination codes on letters;
- Operators at oil refineries to keep the flow of materials through the plant to specification; and
- New staff in the products and services that the organization offers.

Computer-aided learning includes several ways of using the computer:

- Drill and practice
- Tutorials
- Simulation

Each of these is examined in turn in the following sections.

Drill and Practice

Drill-and-practice programs present exercises or problems to learners, who then have to respond to them. For example, a drill-and-practice program for mail sorters who are learning to use electronic sorting machines might operate in the following manner:

- The computer could present a schematic diagram of an addressed envelope;
- Wait until the operator types in a location code; and then
- Either go to the next diagram or show the correct code and explain why it is correct.

Drill-and-practice programs are particularly useful for training in jobs in which there are occasional slow periods and computer equipment is available. For example, this condition occurs in the airline industry, where standby times provide the opportunity for reservation staff to increase skills in taking reservations and knowledge of new products.

Learners can respond to the drill-and-practice program in a number of ways. They might have to type in their answers via a keyboard or they might select from one of a number of multiple-choice options. Drill-and-practice programs are used mainly to support initial training. They are an effective way of building up speed and accuracy of word-processor operators, bank and credit-union tellers, airline-reservation staff, and other employees who use similar sorts of skills.

Tutorials

Tutorial programs can be designed to provide information, test skills and knowledge, and lead learners through a competency area. If a learner should make an error, a tutorial program usually is structured so that it provides revision and retesting. Following are a number of the benefits of using computer-based tutorial programs:

- ♦ They provide information and skills in such a way that the learners are likely to retain them;

- ♦ They are infinitely patient and can be structured so that they give additional, more thorough explanations for learners who are having difficulties;

- ♦ They are also appropriate for fast learners who can demonstrate mastery of a certain area and quickly move to the next unit of work;

- ♦ They do not require the presence of an instructor;

- ♦ They provide immediate feedback;

- ♦ They are an effective way of standardizing training, which is especially important in areas where employees

- need to be licensed or to comply with legislative requirements; and

♦ They can be used after hours so that the normal work day is not disrupted.

Tutorial programs can be used either to introduce or to consolidate a competency area. A computer-based training program can be made up of a number of modular tutorials that cover a range of skills to varying degrees of difficulty. Some tutorial programs that use computer-based training are very sophisticated, but trainers should remember that even small-scale programs developed by those who are learning about computers can be very effective.

Simulation

Computers can be used to provide models of activities, processes, or equipment. In a simulation program, learners can change parameters and see what happens. The program normally consists of a model of a technical system, for example, a processing plant or an aircraft navigation system, and its environment. The learner can practice using the system without the danger of a potentially catastrophic event, such as a plant shutdown or a plane crash.

Military organizations have led the way in designing simulators for missile launchers, aircraft, and battlefields. Many simulators look and respond just as the real thing. For example, flight simulators are correct in every detail, and from the pilot's seat, the learner feels as if he or she is in a real aircraft.

The extent to which a program replicates the real situation is called its *fidelity*. Recently, there has been a trend away from high-fidelity simulators and toward the use of simplified graphic displays to represent work environments, systems, or equipment. Part of the reason for this trend is the high cost of re-creating work environments or technologies, but that is not the only reason. Another important consideration is that to operate a complex technical system, research suggests that one needs to build up an accurate mental model of that system. This mental model need not look like the actual system, but it must function as the actual system does. Simulators that do not try to replicate the real work environment, that is, those that have low fidelity, are probably just as effective as high-fidelity simulators in helping learners to build up a mental model of the system. Often, though, the decision is not between low-fidelity and high-fidelity simulators but about how best to combine low-fidelity simulators, high-fidelity simulators, and on-the-job work experience.

Computer-Managed Learning

In computer-managed learning programs, the computer is used to help the trainer to manage, rather than to directly provide, learning experiences. The distinction between computer-managed learning and computer-aided learning is not always clear. Computer-managed learning may be closely integrated with computer-assisted learning, and a closer integration between these two areas may occur over the next few years. A typical computer-managed learning system has the following three main functions (Figure 10.3):

- Guiding learners through a set of activities;
- Testing learning; and
- Maintaining records of learners' progress and results.

If a learner decides to work through one of a series of modules at work, he or she would typically have to complete a range of activities interspersed with assessment tasks. At the end of the module, the learner would then complete a competency test, and the outcome would have to be recorded.

Figure 10.3. The Differences Between Computer-Managed Learning and Computer-Based Training

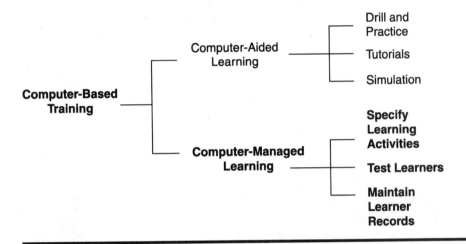

The ways in which computer-managed learning contributes to this process are shown in Figure 10.4. When the learner logs into the system, information is provided about the learning activities that have to be completed. Note that the activities are not usually done directly on the computer. Instead, what shows up on screen and, if necessary, on a printout are checklists and descriptions of what the learner needs to do. Such information might include the following activities:

- Observing and talking with an experienced employee;
- Performing hands-on activities;
- Looking up information in a manual;
- Labeling diagrams;
- Researching information;
- Watching a video; and
- Using a separate computer-based learning program.

Figure 10.4. The Use of Computer-Managed Learning in Skills Training

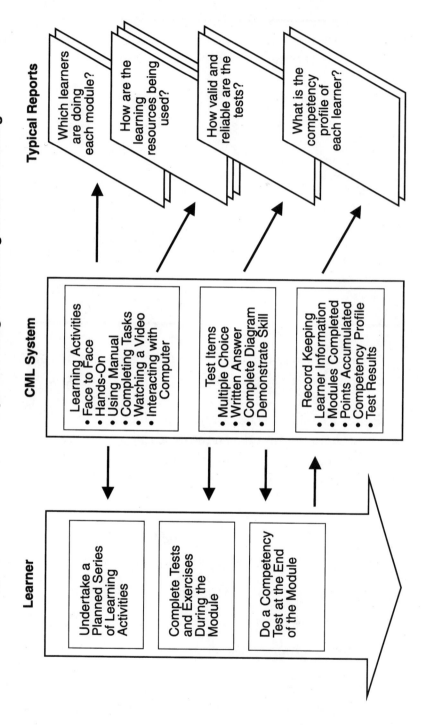

As the learner worked through the module, and again after finishing it, normally he or she would take a test, which could be provided by the computer-managed learning system. For example, if knowledge were being tested, the computer might list multiple-choice questions that could be answered directly using the keyboard or answered on paper and fed into the system via an optical scanner. If task skills were being tested, then the computer might produce a checklist and tell the learner to arrange for an experienced employee to observe the learner's performance of the task.

One of the many benefits of using computer-managed learning is that information can be compiled quickly in a variety of ways to report on such things as the following:

- Which learners are doing each module;
- How learning resources are being used;
- How valid and reliable tests are; and
- What the competency profile of each learner is.

Merits of Computer-Based Learning

Training departments that are considering the use of computer-based training need to understand the merits of this approach in relation to other approaches. Unfortunately there is not any easy way of comparing computer-based training with the other approaches. The choice depends on a range of factors that are related to the following:

- The organization;
- The costs of developing and running the program;
- The learners; and
- The trainers conducting the program.

Some of the main considerations in determining whether computer-based training is useful in a particular situation, are summarized in the following sections.

Organizational Issues

Following are some of the organizational issues that may affect a trainer's decision to use computer-based training:

Batch training. Many organizations postpone training for new employees until they have accumulated enough people to conduct a program. This batch-training approach means that employees can be in an organization for months before they receive basic training in the way the organization operates or in key areas like work safety. Computer-based training can be part of a modular training program that could be made available at any time.

Audience size. Because of elevated development costs, computer-based training is of most use when there are many people who have to do a particular module.

Centralized updating. Training programs that deal with modern technical systems or complex procedures may be difficult to keep up-to-date. Computer-based training can be an effective way of updating training centrally in large organizations or where there is a network of dealerships or franchised agencies.

Travel and accommodation. In organizations that have branches or departments that are spread out, such as motel chains, travel agencies, and health centers, computer-based training can be used to cut down on travel and accommodation costs. And the training that is provided will be of a consistently high standard, no matter where it is offered.

Learner Issues

Following are some of the learner issues that may affect a trainer's decision to use computer-based training:

Self-pacing. Training a group requires that the trainer's pace and level of presentation match that of an average learner. This pace and level can be frustrating for slower learners, who may have difficulty keeping up, as well as for learners who have already mastered the competency area being explained.

Computer-based training programs can be adjusted so that the level of instruction matches the response rates of the individual learners. The level of instruction can be varied in several ways. For example, the computer can be programmed to do the following:

- Change the number of repetitions of each exercise;
- Make choices about going over an area in depth using supplementary exercises or bypassing areas that have already been mastered; or
- Vary the speed at which material is presented.

Satisfaction. A well-designed computer-based training program allows learners to move smoothly through a series of modules covering various competency areas.

No discrimination. Computer-based training programs do not discriminate against different types of learners. Not only are they constant in the way they interact with learners of different ethnic and economic backgrounds, but they are also extremely patient.

Playfulness. Learning programs on the computer can be designed as games, which encourage competition and playfulness. For example, job areas such as marketing can come alive when learners can make decisions in a computer-simulated marketing environment and see the consequences in terms of multimillion-dollar "profits" or "bankruptcy." In addition, different kinds of material may be presented (drill and practice, tutorial, simulation) using a variety of techniques (text, graphics, color, animation, sound) and media (workbooks, videotape, laser videodisc). This quality of playfulness provides a very stimulating environment for the learner.

Availability. In many jobs, such as fire fighting, chemical processing, and cargo handling, employees have periods of idle time. Computer-based training allows some of this time to be used for skill development. In addition, many organizations have to send their employees to other cities for training. Some employees may resent going away for training, and this resentment can be ameliorated by using computer-based training.

User friendliness. There have been rapid developments in recent years in the ease of getting information in and out of computers. These developments are attributable partly to innovations in equipment such as the mouse and the touchscreen and partly to changes in computer programs. These developments and the greater availability of graphic images on screen have resulted in less and less need to rely on the learners' literacy skills. Computers have become much friendlier in recent years, and this trend is sure to continue.

Cost Issues

Following are some of the cost issues that may affect a trainer's decision to use computer-based training:

High development costs. The main limitation of this approach is that initial costs of developing a computer-based program are high (Figure 10.5). The biggest expense is not for equipment but for computer programmers' salaries, and possibly consultants' fees, to design the program and to ensure that

Figure 10.5. Cost-Effectiveness of Computer-Based Training and Classroom Training

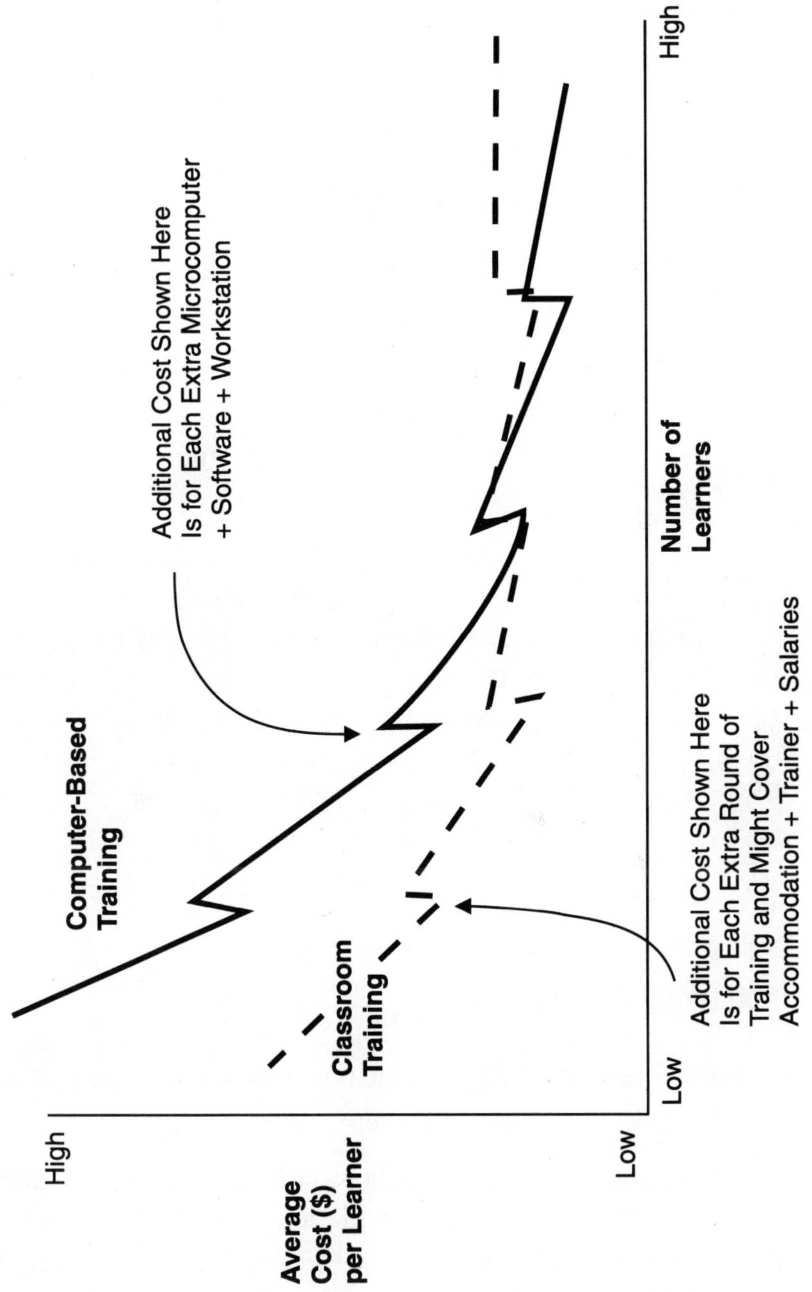

Use Computers in Training

it runs smoothly. For cost reasons, computer-based training is generally feasible only for training areas that have a long life expectancy.

Development time. A major part of the cost of producing a computer-based training program is the time it takes. Although there is a lot of variation in the ratio of development time to instructional time, most accounts cite ratios somewhere between 30 to 1 for simple textual material and 300 to 1 for sophisticated programs using graphics and computer simulation.

Fast skill development. In many situations, computer-based training is a quicker way of developing employee skills than classroom-based training.

Low recurrent costs. Once a program is developed, the costs involved in regularly offering training are quite low. The only significant costs are for computer equipment and software-licensing fees if additional work stations are required. In contrast, classroom training has significant recurrent costs, including accommodation, travel, and trainers' salaries. The difference in recurrent costs will become greater as computer hardware and software become cheaper and the cost of training facilities and staff become greater.

Instructor Issues

Following are some of the instructor issues that may affect a trainer's decision to use computer-based training:

Monitoring. Computers can continually monitor learners' progress and analyze this information to provide a variety of reports. For example, trainers can obtain printouts of the pattern of competencies across a whole group of learners and can easily identify parts of a module that learners are finding difficult.

Safe training. In many workplaces, individuals cannot operate systems unless they are highly skilled. For example, in computer-integrated manufacturing, aircraft piloting, and materials processing, a small error could have disastrous results. Even in workplaces where using technology is encouraged, learners do not always have sufficient access to the technology to develop their skill levels. Computer-based training allows learning to take place safely and with as much practice as necessary.

Heuristic thinking. Heuristic thinking is the type of thinking that is done when people are contemplating new ideas, acting on hunches, and exploring cause-and-effect relationships. Heuristic thinking is very important for the development of under-the-surface skills. It can be developed more effectively via computers than by using more linear media such as videotapes or workbooks.

Testing skills in finding errors or malfunctions. Trainers would find it difficult to develop a paper-and-pen test of error-finding skills that replicates a computer-integrated database or control system. Computer-based training offers a way of testing error-finding skills on computer-integrated systems such as these. Because the system model stored in the training computer can be the same as the workplace computer's system model, realistic scenarios can be developed.

Optimize training quality. In classroom training, some learners will have better trainers than others. Computer-based training allows the best trainers and technical experts to work together to provide consistently first-class training programs.

Reduce administrative work. Programs that help trainers to manage the training program handle most of the routine, and possibly tedious, work. If used properly, computer-based training can leave more time for trainers to be involved in educational rather than clerical duties.

Computers and Interactive Video

Even though the use of computers in training has enormous potential, many computer-aided learning programs fail to use this potential fully. A learner who has to sit for long periods in front of a computer monitor that shows only text will lose interest after a short time. Even computer-generated graphics cannot compare with live action, and this fact accounts for the recent upsurge of interest in interactive video.

The term *interactive video* refers to the use of any video system in which the sequence and selection of images is to some extent determined by the learner's responses. The video system can be either videotape or laser videodisc, but laser videodisc is likely to become the more popular medium (Figure 10.6). Laser videodiscs are shiny disks that look like a large version of a compact disc. The audiovisual information that is stored on the videodisc is read by a laser beam in the videodisc player and can be shown on an ordinary television or computer monitor.

Figure 10.6. The Main Components of a Typical Interactive Video System

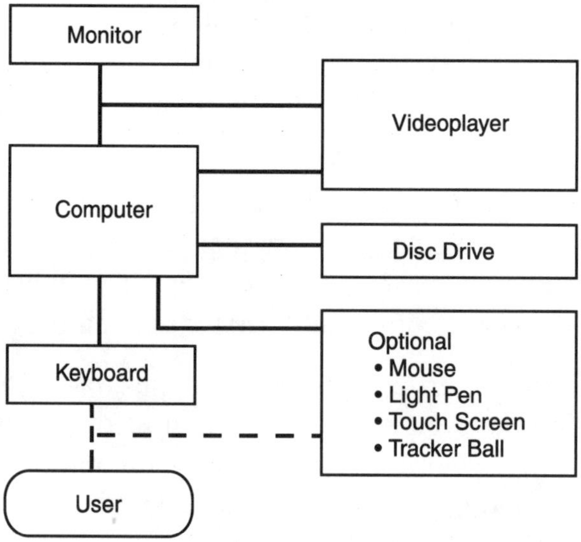

Laser videodisc has a certain number of advantages over videotape:

Random access. Videodiscs can retrieve a still or moving image quickly, regardless of where it is on the disk;

Durability. Videodiscs are more durable than videotapes;

Flexibility. Videodiscs produce high-quality images in fast motion, slow motion, or fixed frame.

For these reasons, laser videodisc is a far more effective medium for interactive training programs than videotape. Videodisc can be used in a skills-training program in five different ways (Figure 10.7).

Applications of Interactive Video

In recent years, interactive video has been used successfully for training a wide range of employees:

- Aviation mechanics
- Refinery operators
- Retail store personnel
- Nurses
- Army artillery personnel
- Postal workers
- Automotive workers
- Bank tellers

Training programs for these and similar groups cover all the different areas of computer-aided learning, that is, drill and practice, tutorials, and simulations. Some specific applications are included on the following page:

Figure 10.7. Levels of Interaction in Training Programs

Level of Interaction	Meaning
1. Passive	No interaction other than the learner switching equipment on and off.
2. Spectator	The learner can only indicate when he or she is ready to go on to the next image.
3. Selective Spectator	The learner can choose his or her own route through the module using a menu of options.
4. Participant	Same as 3, but with the facility for branching options.
5. Fully Interactive	Full continuous interaciton, as occurs, for example, in a simulator with changing parameters in response to learner input.

- Health and safety procedures brought about by new legislation;
- New products and services;
- The operation of technical systems;
- Maintenance work on high-technology equipment;
- Use of databases;
- Operation of customer accounts; and
- The procedures to be followed in a franchise business.

Merits of Interactive Video

To fully appreciate the benefits of interactive video, trainers should see it in operation in a training facility or at a computer exhibition. If seeing it is not possible, then the trainers will have to visualize a typical application.

One such application might be a program designed to train an automotive mechanic in how to adjust a fuel injector. On the screen is a realistic image of a fuel injector, accompanied by the sound of an idling engine. The learner adjusts the fuel injector using a light pen. As the adjustment is being made, there are realistic changes in the sound of the engine, and a display shows what happens to revs and fuel consumption. If extra help is needed, the learner can skip to a video sequence that shows an experienced mechanic in the act of making the adjustment correctly.

As this example illustrates, the relationship between learner and computer-based training using interactive video is similar to the relationship between apprentice and skilled employee: The learner has the opportunity to practice a skill over and over again and to ask questions that result in detailed demonstrations and explanations.

Apart from its similarity to the time-honored tradition of the master-apprentice relationship, interactive video has a number of other advantages:

Realistic images. In contrast to computer text or graphics, interactive video images are very realistic. There are many areas of training in which the trainer will find it difficult to present the skill in any way other than visually. Not only can interactive video make a visual presentation, but it can also slow a movement down (or speed it up) and repeat the same demonstration as many times as necessary. The ability to repeat a demonstration is particularly important for tasks that involve unusual cues or difficult coordination between what the eyes have to do and the hands have to do.

Relationships between system components. In learning about complex data or control systems, learners might take a long time to understand how all the parts fit together. Laser videodisc enables learners to explore networks of relationships easily.

Inexpensive simulation. Simulators that try to replicate real pieces of equipment or work environments usually are expensive. Interactive video can simulate these environments much more inexpensively. Sometimes the training solution that best balances effectiveness and cost considerations is to use interactive video to establish procedures and routines and then to use a simulator or the actual piece of equipment to give learners a realistic feel for the job.

Interactive video also has some limitations:

Cost. The initial cost of developing a "master" video is very high. However, once a master video is produced, duplicating multiple copies is relatively inexpensive. Costs are also coming down as a result of the development of WORM (Write Once, Read Many) disks that can be produced in-house.

Shortage of programs. The range of vocational training disks that can be bought off-the-shelf is limited, although this situation is gradually changing.

Personnel. Whether interactive video programs are developed within industry, a lot of outside help will still be needed. For example, a typical program might require instructional designers, script writers, computer-based training experts, video producers, and subject-matter experts.

Resistance to Computer-Based Training

Trainers who have looked into computer-based training and decided to press for its introduction can expect to meet a certain amount of resistance from other trainers and from management. Resistance to any change is inevitable and it needs to be understood and countered if improvements are to occur. The main reasons for resistance to computer-based training are as follows:

"I can't understand it." Trainers may be reluctant to support computer-based training out of a fear of the unknown. It is

possible that a common element in the psychological makeup of many trainers is that they do not like to feel "ignorant." After all, the role of trainer carries a kind of buffer against ignorance—trainers are normally in situations in which they are more knowledgeable and more skilled than the learners. Although trainers may find many reasons for not wanting to become involved in computer-based training, these reasons may simply be rationalizations for fear of the unknown.

"I've been through this before and none of the other programs have worked." Part of the resistance may be related to the view that other technologies have failed to live up to their promise so computer-based training probably will not be any different. Programmed instruction, black-and-white reel-to-reel video, and other technologies that were used in training have come and gone, and so, say the critics, will computer-based training.

There is some truth in this viewpoint. Computer-based training is in a state of evolution and it will no doubt be superseded by advances that are being developed at present. These advances include the following:

- Better visual displays using animation and three-dimensional images;
- More flexible interaction methods, for example, devices that track eye and hand movements and voice input;
- Better integration of programs, media, image types, and databases; and
- An enhanced ability to do multiple tasks on multiple screens.

Nevertheless, the fact that the present technologies will inevitably be superseded is no reason to avoid using computer-based training, as long as it is seen as just one component of training. Computer-based training is certainly not a panacea for curing skill deficiencies, but, judging by the experience of organizations that have used it, it has a great deal to offer if properly integrated with personal contact and other instructional approaches.

"I can't see the benefits." Part of the resistance may be associated with caution about the tangible organizational benefits of introducing computer-based training. This concern is valid one. Trainers who are trying to get support for computer-based training need to remember that no matter how stylish a training program is, the real measure of its success should be the extent to which it contributes to the formation of skills and to results in the workplace.

"I'll be out of a job!" The worry is sometimes expressed that computer-based training and related technologies will replace trainers. There is no evidence to support this fear. In fact, the experience of organizations that have adopted computer-based training suggests that the effectiveness of these programs is dependent on the trainers' abilities. Successful use of computer-based training hinges on the quality of human effort more than anything else.

If the trainer is trying to encourage the involvement of colleagues in computer-based training, he or she will need to provide support before, during, and after it is introduced. As with any significant change, phasing in computer-based training is preferable to introducing it as the primary training method across a whole organization overnight.

Bibliography

Bijlstra, J., & Jelsma, O. (1988). Some thoughts on interactive video as a training tool for process operators. *PLET,* 25(1).

Burns, I., Stubbs, N., & Leavesley, J. (1987). *Computer-based training: Case studies.* Canberra, Australia: National Training Council.

Dean, C., & Whitlock, Q. (1983). *A handbook of computer-based training*. London: Kogan Page.

Duchastel, P. (1988). Models for AI in education and training. In P. Ercoli and R. Lewis (Eds.), *Artificial intelligence tools in education*. Amsterdam: Elsevier Science.

Further Education Unit. (1987). *Information technology support systems for education and training*. London: Author.

Further Education Unit. (1989). *The key technologies: Some implications for education and training*. London: Author.

Griffiths, M. (1986). Interactive video at work. *PLET, 23*(3).

Jennings, C., & Ayerst, J. (1989). *Criteria for the selection of generic courseware*. London: The National Interactive Video Centre.

Kearsley, G. (1983). *Computer based training: A guide to selection and implementation*. Reading, MA: Addison Wesley.

Kearsley, G., & Hillelsohn, M. (1982). Human factors considerations for computer based training. *Journal of Computer Based Instruction, 8*(4).

Langer, V. (1987, Spring). Developing a computer-integrated manufacturing education centre. In I. Charner & C. Rolzinski, (Eds.), *Responding to the educational needs of today's workplace* (Higher Education Sourcebook Series No. 33). San Francisco, CA: Jossey-Bass.

Morris, R. (1980). Using computer assisted training to learn how to locate faults. In R. Winterburn and L. Evans (Eds.), *Aspects of educational technology* (Vol. XIV). London: Kogan Page.

Palmer, R. (1988). *Designing and using CBT interactive video*. Manchester, UK: National Computing Centre.

Pogrow, S. (1988, May/June). How to use computers to truly enhance learning. *Electronic Learning*.

Learning modules are like stepping stones of different sizes and varying composition

Modular Training

Modular training is attracting a lot of interest, and many companies and industry groups have developed, or are attempting to develop, modular approaches to support a new award structure emphasizing skill formation. These modular programs are sometimes intended for in-house use or as part of programs offered by high schools.

A module is a specific learning segment, complete in itself, that deals with one or a number of competencies to a particular standard. A modular training program consists of a series of modules that may be completed either one at a time or simultaneously. Learning modules are like stepping stones of different sizes and varying composition. By completing a number of modules, a learner covers new competency areas and can gradually complete a whole training program.

There are a number of reasons for the increased interest in modular training:

- Material is presented in selected portions that are easy to assimilate;
- Learners and trainers can choose the areas to address;
- Learners are provided with a way of conveniently building up skills; and

♦ Modules that deal with changing competency areas can be updated regularly without affecting the rest of the program.

Given the newness of this training approach within many organizations and training centers, there is an increased need for trainers to understand modular training.

Chapter 11 begins by defining the term *module* and describing the nature of modular training programs. A distinction is made between a modular approach and individualized instruction. It is emphasized that although many modular programs consist of self-paced modules, self-pacing is not a necessary characteristic of modular training.

The chapter also discusses self-paced modular programs and assesses the merits of this approach for learners and trainers. It then discusses the format of learner guides, which are often provided for each module. Finally, the chapter offers some suggestions regarding the introduction of modular training.

Modules and Modular Programs

Modules

A module is a complete, specific learning segment that deals with one or a number of competencies to a particular standard. A module is capable of being assessed separately and may either stand on its own or be linked to other modules in the same or related study areas.

Note that this definition does not imply any particular method of teaching or learning. A module basically refers to a way of dividing and assessing content. There are a range of instructional approaches that can accompany modular training. Although many modular programs use self-pacing and individualized instruction, these methods are not associated necessarily with modular training.

Modular Programs

A modular training program consists of a series of modules that may be completed either one at a time or simultaneously. A wide range of training approaches used in industry could be called "modular"; consequently, it is not possible to offer a strict definition of a modular structure. Usually, however, a modular program can be described as follows:

- Supported by a trainer who is primarily a facilitator rather than a source of information;

- Composed of a range of media (print, video, computer simulation, audiovisual) to provide variety and motivation;

- Designed to recognize and give credit or exemptions for skills that have already been mastered;

- Linked to continual assessment, which consists partly of learners' checking their own progress and partly of formal assessments by trainers or experienced employees; and

- Composed of individual modules that can be combined in a variety of patterns to provide a learner with flexibility in terms of specialization or multiskilling.

The ways in which modules fit together to make up a modular program vary considerably. A common modular pattern for entry-level training within some industries consists of *broad-based modules* that cover the common core for several vocational areas, followed by specialized modules for trade and post-trade levels (Figure 11.1). Within this overall framework there is considerable flexibility. Colleges can offer modules in many different patterns, such as weekend courses, twenty two-hour sessions, or any other pattern that suits that industry and the module content. Modules can be done one at a time or several

Figure 11.1. A Modular Program for an Industry

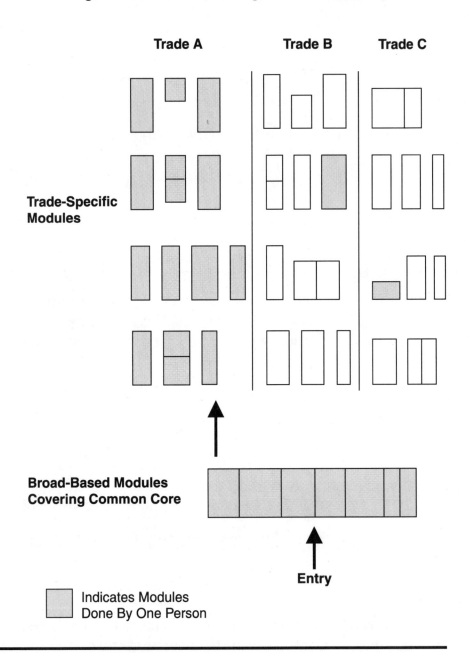

can be done in parallel, and they incorporate a range of instructional approaches.

Modular programs are useful for many different kinds of training purposes. They can be offered at colleges, at high schools, at industry-skills centers, or on-site within individual organizations.

Self-Paced Modules

The last section pointed out that the term *modular program* does not refer to any particular instructional approach. Nevertheless, modules are often designed so that a learner can study each module at his or her own pace and can do most the work alone or at least without the presence of a trainer. The introduction of self-paced modules has implications for learners and trainers. The following sections discuss how self-pacing affects learners and trainers.

Learners and Self-Pacing

As discussed in Chapter 3, learning is like trying to navigate through uncharted territory. Some people can persist and are good at finding their way through the difficulties, whereas others quickly give up. The skill that is needed here is *self-directed learning,* which is part of the skill area of *workplace learning.*

Most adults have some skills at self-directed learning, but research has shown that these skills can be developed further. Self-directed learning skills are important for a number of reasons:

Developing the quality of being self-directed is one goal of personal growth and development. By encouraging learners to take risks and explore new areas on their own, self-paced modules can contribute to their personal growth.

Employees learn a lot of their skills on the job. In fact, some studies suggest as much as 80 percent of the skills employees use in their day-to-day work are learned on the job. Employees learn by actively seeking what they need from other employees or from job aids such as technical manuals. Self-paced modules encourage this natural process.

There is evidence that the quality of being self-directed helps individuals to overcome educational barriers. The encouragement of self-directed learning skills can provide an opportunity for employees with poor educational backgrounds to increase their education.

On the other hand, the emphasis that modular training places on being self-directed can have its drawbacks for learners. With any group, there is a range from individuals who are very self-directed to those who are not motivated easily or who are distracted easily. Self-paced modular training may not be suitable for individuals at either end of this range. Some learners may not find the modules challenging enough, and they may need additional exercises that are more difficult. Slower learners or those who are underskilled may find the modules' emphasis on self-direction too frustrating.

Self-paced modules may also not be suitable for learners with poor literacy skills. The printed material and the exercises requiring written answers that usually are part of a module are normally targeted to an "average" learner and this level of presentation can pose difficulties for employees who meet the following criteria:

- Cannot read or write the language used in the printed material;
- Are poor spellers; and
- Are afraid that their illiteracy may be discovered.

Finally, some work environments are not conducive to self-paced, individualized study. Some learners may have too many distractions during work time, and they may find it difficult to work effectively if they are doing shift work. The culture of some industries is such that employees are encouraged to work in groups, and a group emphasis may make learning difficult for individuals who are studying various modules at different rates.

Trainers and Self-Pacing

The introduction of self-paced modules requires a change in the role of the trainer. The new role combines flexibility with active involvement and is more concerned with facilitation than with instruction.

Self-paced modules provide a trainer with an opportunity to get to know learners personally. A lot of the discussion is one-to-one in a self-paced modular program, and this approach provides an opportunity to establish rapport. A self-paced approach also has the advantage that the trainer can check each learner's work individually, which increases the likelihood that the assessment is accurate.

But trainers also need to be aware of the difficulties that may accompany the introduction of self-paced modules:

- ♦ The trainer may find it more difficult to keep track of assessment results than he or she would in a traditional program. A number of organizations are using computer-managed learning systems in an attempt to deal with this problem. These systems can operate on a personal computer and are accessible to both the learner and the trainer.

- ♦ Learners who fail to complete a module satisfactorily may present problems for the trainer. Before introducing a self-paced modular program, a trainer needs to think carefully about how failure will be handled.

- A trainer may need to work hard to achieve group cohesiveness while working with individuals. In many ways, self-paced modules result in more work than traditional training, and the notion that self-paced training is easy for the trainer is incorrect.

- A trainer has less control with a self-paced modular program than he or she would have with a traditional program, and having less control can feel quite threatening to the trainer.

Learner Guides

In most modular training programs, notes are provided for each module to guide learners through the various exercises and assessment tasks. These notes are called *learner guides.*

Learner guides are available in a variety of formats, including booklets and loose-leaf folders. Regardless of format differences, all learner guides are structured in much the same way. Following is a description of a typical structure for a learner guide:

- Title
- Introduction
- Target audience
- Objectives
- Prerequisite skills and knowledge
- Resources
- Learning activities
- Self-assessment
- Formal competency assessment

A discussion on what each of these sections might cover follows.

Title. The module title is usually the competency or competency area that the module explains, for example, "Adjusting a Carburetor" or "Selecting Typefaces."

Introduction. The introduction describes what the module is about and shows how it is related to other parts of the program. The introduction should also indicate in general terms what learners will be able to do when they have completed the module.

Target audience. The learner guide should state the audience for whom this module is designed, for example, "Second-year dental technicians who have completed skills modules A, B, and C."

Objectives. The objectives indicate what learners are expected to know and what they should be able to do once they have completed the module. Learner guides usually include the conditions under which the assessment will take place and the assessment standards. However, the trainer will need to decide how detailed to make the objectives, and in some competency areas it may not be appropriate to be too prescriptive. For example, in an area such as finding errors or malfunctions, the desirable standard may be "as well as possible," rather than something more precise and measurable.

Prerequisite skills and knowledge. This section of the learner guide states what skills and knowledge the learners should have before starting the module. There may be a module pretest to make sure that learners meet these prerequisites or a list of the modules that should be completed before the learners can begin the module at hand. This section should also indicate how learners who do not satisfy the prerequisites can acquire what they need.

Resources. The resources that are needed for the module are usually listed in the guide. Resources might include people, tools, equipment, systems, software, raw materials, practical workshops, audiovisual materials, and reference manuals. The resource list is handy for the trainer as well as the learner; by referring to the list, they can make sure that everything they need is available before starting a module.

Learning activities. The learner guide describes the various activities, in sequence, that the learner needs to perform in order to complete the module. These activities might include the following:

- Looking up and reading information in a reference manual;
- Visiting a plant and jotting down particular information or sketching components, flow directions, and settings;
- Performing a task and recording the results;
- Asking an experienced employee a series of questions and recording his or her answers;
- Watching a videotape or interacting with a laser videodisc program;
- Attending formal classroom training;
- Using a computer-simulated program;
- Performing competencies on-site and under supervision and asking a supervisor to provide written verification of the competencies performed; and
- Asking a trainer to demonstrate a task.

Self-assessment. Learner guides usually contain exercises so that learners can test themselves from time to time as they work through the module. The purpose of these exercises is to provide learners with feedback so they can tell whether or not they are mastering the necessary skills and knowledge. Most of the learning experiences listed in the last paragraph could have answers or assessment criteria supplied so that learners can check their progress.

Formal competency assessment. At the end of the module, a learner would usually have a formal assessment. For task skills, this assessment might involve demonstrating the task in front of a trainer or in-house assessment committee. Assessment of routine procedures is easier if a checklist such as a competency guide (see Chapter 4 for details) is used.

For competencies that are not tasks, an assessment may be more difficult. For example, a demonstration might not be a suitable approach for assessing competencies that involve danger or that are associated with unusual circumstances, such as a system shutdown. Approaches to competency assessment are discussed more fully in Chapter 14.

Introducing Modular Training

Like any training initiative, plans to modularize training need to be thought about in terms of the sorts of factors that were discussed in Chapter 1: Whether or not modular training is appropriate might depend on the industry, the skills that have to be developed, the nature of the technology, organizational attitudes toward learning, the support of unions, the degree to which the learner is self-directed and the learner's ability to read and write.

If, as a result of investigating these issues and talking with a cross section of the people affected, the trainer decides to adopt modular training he or she can increase the likelihood that the new program approach is successfully implemented by doing the following:

Building flexibility into the materials. For example, the notes that accompany a module can gradually be assembled into a folder, along with sheets provided by the trainer and the learner's own samples and notes. At the completion of each module, the learner then has his or her own tailor-made package that can be referred to in the workplace. If possible, learners who speak different languages should be able to do module exercises in their native languages.

Modules can also be made more flexible with the provision of alternative activities that can accommodate different equipment, learner abilities, and previous knowledge or experience on the part of learners.

Ensuring that there is support for the introduction of modular training. As with any change, the trainer needs to recognize that different people in an organization have very different concerns. Although the trainer may be committed to modules as an effective way to solve particular training problems, others in the organization may not realize that these problems even exist. Therefore, those who will be expected to support the use of the modules (perhaps even prospective trainers) will need to be involved in planning from the start.

Similar issues arise if experienced employees are expected to help learners complete modules at the workplace. Initial training and ongoing support will need to be provided for employees expected to conduct such on-the-job training (see Chapter 9 for details).

Piloting modules before they are finalized. To *pilot* means to try out the materials with typical groups of users and to obtain their help in pinpointing anything that is unhelpful or unclear. Piloting the materials is also a way of starting to cultivate the support of trainers for the new modular materials.

Aiming for clarity, accuracy, and simplicity. The trainer should make sure that the written material is not too difficult for learners and that the style of writing is coherent and straightforward. Technical content needs to be checked to ensure that it is up-to-date, and the wording should be checked to ensure that it is not offensive to any particular gender or group.

Bibliography

Finch, C., & Crunkilton, J. (1979). *Curriculum development in vocational and technical education.* Boston, MA: Allyn and Bacon.

Wells, C. (1981). *Student assessment and progression problems in modular trade courses.* Sydney: TAFE Assessment Research & Development Unit.

Demonstrations can take place on equipment and systems the learners are familiar with

Explaining and Demonstrating a Task

A trainer often has to explain what is involved in a particular task and support the explanation with a demonstration. In some organizations, sessions like this take place in a classroom, and the trainer uses samples, equipment, test instruments, computer terminals, charts, and other training aids to demonstrate the task. In other organizations, the training session is conducted in the actual work environment or in a simulated version of it. The explanation and demonstration can then take place on the actual equipment or systems that learners are familiar with.

This chapter covers the basic techniques of combining explanations with hands-on demonstrations within a training session. It describes the rationale for supplementing explanations with demonstrations and gives advice about how to apply adult-learning principles to the process of explanation and demonstration. The things that need to be done to prepare for the training session are discussed, and the chapter explains how to write and structure a lesson plan for a session that combines explanation with demonstration.

Purpose of Combining Explanation and Demonstration

In many types of training dealing with physical actions and routine skills, a trainer has to combine an explanation with a demonstration of how to perform a task. One way of structuring such a lesson is as follows:

- The trainer puts the task in context by explaining where it fits in the job and what it involves.
- The trainer demonstrates how to perform the task.
- The trainer repeats the demonstration slowly.
- A learner attempts the task in front of the class, with help from other learners and from the trainer.
- All the learners attempt the task.
- The trainer demonstrates any common difficulties to all the learners.
- All the learners complete the task.

As this example illustrates, the demonstration is a very important part of practical instruction, especially in the early stages of mastering a competency.

A good demonstration does several things:

- It shows learners step-by-step exactly what they have to do and how each step fits into the overall task.
- It provides a model to copy so that learners can begin to understand what steps are important, what parts are difficult, and how to check whether they are using the correct method.
- It links physical activities to knowledge and attitudes. Even routine, physical tasks require knowledge ("What setting do I need now?") and attitudes ("Should I bother

to grind some more off?"). The demonstration makes the physical actions explicit and links them to the necessary knowledge and attitudes.

Adult Learning and the Demonstration Session

In recent years, there has been a lot of research done into adult learners and learning. This research suggests the following about adult learners:

- They become ready to learn when they recognize deficiencies in their own skills and accept that they need to take action to remedy these deficiencies.
- They want learning to be problem based, leading to the solution of particular problems facing the individual. In training terms, there must be a clear "need to know."
- They want to be treated as adults, enjoying the respect of the trainer and of other learners, and to have the experiences that they bring with them accepted as valid.
- Each adult learner brings to the learning situation his or her own unique mixture of characteristics:
  - Self-confidence, self-esteem, and self-image;
  - Learning style and pace of learning;
  - Physical state, complete with acquired impairments; and
  - Personality.

These findings have important implications for how and when trainers conduct demonstrations in a training session. These implications are related to the following five factors:

- Meaningfulness

- Prerequisites
- Modeling
- Novelty
- Clarity

In this section, each of these factors is discussed.

Meaningfulness

People are more likely to be motivated to learn if training relates to and adds to the skills that they already have. Of course, their backgrounds, jobs, and interests will vary, so it may not always be possible to make every aspect of the training meaningful to everyone. But the trainer can increase the likelihood that the training will be meaningful by doing the following:

- Linking the demonstration to the skills that learners have already acquired;
- Encouraging learners to understand the techniques being demonstrated in relation to practices on-the-job so that they can see clearly how these techniques can be applied.
- Linking the area that is being discussed session to broader systems or processes. For example, in organizations using computer-based technologies, it is important that learners gradually build up an understanding of the systems and the way in which people's tasks interrelate with the system components.

Prerequisites

People are more likely to learn something if they have mastered all the preliminary competencies, that is, the prerequisites. If the trainer overlooks this fact, then learners will become frustrated.

The trainer can keep such frustration from developing by doing the following:

- Beginning the demonstration by testing the learners' present skills and knowledge. This testing can be done by administering a quiz or by demonstrating the necessary skills or tasks and then asking learners to identify the cues they would respond to at each step and what they would do next.

- Providing bridging modules so that learners who do not meet the prerequisites can gain necessary skills and knowledge.

- Dividing the session into small groups according to the learners' abilities or degrees of mastery and giving particular emphasis to prerequisites when demonstrating to less experienced learners.

Modeling

People are more likely to become competent if they are presented with a model performance to watch and imitate. This principle is the foundation of the session for explanation and demonstration.

A trainer can increase his or her effectiveness as a model by doing the following:

- Checking equipment, tools, and the demonstration procedure beforehand to make sure everything needed is available and in working order.

- Proceeding step-by-step through the task being demonstrated and avoiding the temptation to take shortcuts.

- Observing all safety precautions.

- Working to standards that are realistic for learners to achieve and that are acceptable on the job. For some tasks, the trainer may not be able to achieve these two aims. If that is the case, the demonstration should be done twice: once to show normal industry standards and then a second time to show a standard that learners can achieve.

- Admitting mistakes. If something goes wrong during the demonstration, the trainer should admit it and either go through the procedure again or, if that is not possible, show what should have happened.

Novelty

People are more likely to learn if their attention is attracted by presentations that are new and varied. This does not imply that the trainer should tell jokes during the whole session, but that the trainer should try to make a demonstration interesting. Novelty in a demonstration can be achieved by doing the following:

- Using teaching aids and methods that stimulate a variety of senses. Appeal to the learners' senses of smell, touch, and hearing and not only their sense of seeing. Some examples are shown in Figure 12.1.

- Avoiding time-wasting delays like waiting for machines to warm up, accessing computer networks, or loading software by getting ready beforehand and by preparing samples of the task or product as it appears at different stages.

- Varying the pace and structure of the session by setting time aside for questions, discussion, and practice. Learners' interest is heightened when they are able to take part actively in the demonstration by either copying the

Figure 12.1. Training Aids That Stimulate the Senses

Sense		Example
Smell		Learners distinguish between the smell of fresh and burnt oil.
Touch		Learners feel the surface of a defective plastic moulding.
Hearing		Learners listen to the sound of poorly fitted shock absorbers.

trainer step-by-step or by attempting the task under the trainer's supervision.

♦ Inviting technical experts and equipment suppliers to demonstrate the latest techniques and hardware.

Clarity

People are more likely to learn if what the trainer says and does is clear. The trainer can aid clarity by doing the following:

♦ Beginning each session with a clear statement of objectives so that the learners know what to watch for and what they will need to remember and do after the session.

Explaining and Demonstrating a Task

- Pointing out the cues that are acted on and the decisions that are made at each step in the demonstration. The trainer also should let learners know about the under-the-surface skills that are used.

- Checking learners' understanding by asking questions at regular intervals during the demonstration.

- Exaggerating small movements. Unless the trainer highlights it, a small movement can easily be missed no matter how well it is demonstrated.

- Slowing down when demonstrating complex moves. A rushed demonstration is difficult to follow, especially if it contains a number of movements. The aim of the demonstration is to train, not to complete a task as quickly as possible.

- Avoiding unnecessary movements. Every movement in the demonstration is liable to be imitated by learners. Therefore, the trainer should avoid unnecessary movements that could be copied by learners.

- Keeping the explanations brief and trying to avoid talking too much while demonstrating the skills or tasks.

Preparing for the Session

Following are some of the things that need to be done before conducting a session of explanation and demonstration:

- Research the task.
- Gauge the learners' abilities and the current levels of development.
- Check the facilities.
- Write performance objectives.

- Structure the training session.
- Prepare a lesson plan.
- Prepare training aids.

Each of these activities is discussed in the following sections. In several cases, references are given to more detailed coverage in other chapters.

Research the task. The trainer will need to do some research beforehand if he or she is not completely familiar with the task. For example, the research might involve understanding a brand of equipment that the trainer has not used before or a new type of raw material. The trainer should seek advice from others who do have firsthand experience and, if necessary, carry out a simple task analysis (see Chapter 4 for details).

Gauge learners' skills. The session will be more effective if it is related to the difficulties that learners have had, to their capabilities, and to their previous activities. This means that the trainer needs to avoid the temptation to base the session on his or her own level of skills; instead, the session should be based on the group's level, and the trainer should avoid showing off or talking down to learners.

Check the facilities. Do not just assume that the training room is set up or that equipment is working properly. Limited access to machinery or materials will influence what the trainer can do. For example, if an overhead projector is not available, then the trainer cannot use his or her overhead transparencies; if the facility is to be shared with another group that is doing noisy work, then the trainer may not be able to give a complex demonstration.

Write performance objectives. Think about what learners will be required to do during and after the training session, for example, "Learners will be able to demonstrate the correct procedures for injection and extraction of resin transfer moldings." Notice that this statement defines what the learners should be able to do rather than what the trainer must do (see Chapter 6 for details).

Structure the training session. The trainer needs to plan the overall training strategy, which should include how the demonstration is to be structured and where practice will occur (see Chapter 8 for details).

Prepare a lesson plan. The lesson plan indicates what the objectives of the lesson are and what tools, equipment, and materials are needed. Usually, it also shows what learners have to do (tasks and steps) and what they have to know or respond to (key points or cues). Lesson-plan formats are discussed in the next section.

Prepare training aids. Training aids include overhead transparencies, computer simulations (see Chapter 10 for details), charts, videotapes, videodiscs, and models. The main points to consider when making or selecting training aids are as follows:

- Clarity: Will the learners be able to see the aid clearly? Does it make its point clearly?
- Relevance: Does the aid make a point relevant to the session? Are the terms used in the same way that the learners' organization uses them?
- Usefulness: Is it easy to use?

If the answer to most of these questions is yes, then the job aids are probably worth using.

Conducting the Session

Before planning a session for explanation and demonstration, the trainer will need to think about how to structure the lesson and make sure that the learners are comfortable. A good demonstration lesson contains three stages: an introduction, the body, and a conclusion. The main aspects of each stage and how to ensure an appropriate learning environment are discussed in this section.

No matter how well a demonstration is based on the principles of learning, it will be ineffective if learners cannot see and hear the trainer, are physically uncomfortable, or are subjected to repeated distractions. Therefore, the trainer should do the following:

- Make sure learners are physically comfortable during the demonstration. For example, check heating and ventilation, and plan to avoid long periods of standing.

- Arrange the demonstration to make sure that all learners can see and hear clearly. For example, to demonstrate fine adjustments to a large piece of machinery, the trainer may need to use a video camera mounted over the machine so that the class can view the procedure on a television monitor.

- Minimize distracting influences, such as noisy machinery and the activities of other learners. If distractions like noise cannot be avoided, the trainer will need to develop a strategy to get the information across in spite of them. For example, the trainer could use a microphone and a portable receiver/amplifier. This equipment would allow the trainer to demonstrate the task at a normal voice level but still be heard over the noise.

Introduction

During the introduction to the session, the trainer should do the steps listed on the following page:

- Interest learners by connecting the demonstration to previous work and to what they will be required to do subsequently;
- Show learners why they need to be able to perform a task;
- State the theme or title of the session;
- Review relevant work that has been done previously;
- State the session objective; and
- Discuss the scope of the session.

The trainer can remember these six steps easily by using some of the letters of the word "introductions":

- Interest
- Need
- Title
- Review
- Objectives
- Scope

Body

During the body of the session, the trainer should do the following items:

- Avoid taking shortcuts when demonstrating how to do the task;
- Observe all safety precautions;
- Work to standards that are realistic for learners to achieve but are also acceptable in the workplace;
- Tell learners what cues are being acted on;

- Check learners' understanding by asking questions;
- Avoid talking down to learners;
- Avoid time wasting delays by getting ready beforehand and by using previously prepared samples; and
- Vary the pace and structure of the session.

Conclusion

During the conclusion to the session, the trainer should do the following:

- Review the main points of the training session;
- Distribute handouts containing exercises and reference information; and
- Remind learners when they will get an opportunity to practice performing the task or applying the skills.

Planning the Session

The format used to plan the session for explanation and demonstration is partly a matter of personal preference. The plan format should make it easy for the trainer to follow the intended sequence of ideas and steps to achieve his or her objectives.

In most situations, session plans should do the following:

- Identify the session, the learners, the time of the session, and the date;
- Indicate specifically what is to be covered;
- List which tasks learners should be able to perform at the end of the session;

- Itemize the materials that are needed in order to conduct the demonstration;

- Indicate which textbooks and which competency guides are related to the session;

- Indicate how the explanation and demonstration will be linked with previous learnings and how the trainer will gain the learners' interest.

- Remind the trainer when to ask questions and use training aids;

- List what the trainer intends to do. The list might include the steps, tasks, or operations involved and the main points that need to be highlighted;

- Indicate where practice is to take place; and

- State what needs to be emphasized in the conclusion.

Bibliography

Davis, L. (1974). *Planning, conducting, and evaluating workshops.* Austin, TX: Learning Concepts.

Davis, R., Alexander, L., & Yelon, S. (1974). *Learning system design.* New York: McGraw-Hill.

Gagne, R., Briggs, L., & Wager, W. (1988). *Principles of instructional design.* New York: Holt, Rinhart & Winston.

Knowles, M. (1985). *Andragogy in action.* San Francisco, CA: Jossey-Bass.

Knox, A. (1987). *Helping adults learn.* San Francisco, CA: Jossey-Bass.

Laird, D. (1985). *Approaches to training and development.* Reading, MA: Addison-Wesley.

Newman, M. (1986). *Tutoring adults.* Melbourne: Council of Adult Education. (A set of six booklets).

Rose, H. (1966). *The instructor and his job.* Chicago: American Technical Society.

Sork, T. (Ed.). (1984). *Designing and implementing effective workshops.* San Francisco, CA: Jossey-Bass.

These welds are nice and strong...but you'll need to change the angles a little...

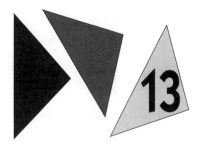

Supervise Practice

Supervised practice is one of the most important aspects of skills training. Workplace skills may be practiced in a variety of locations:

- In a classroom equipped with computer terminals or testing apparatus;
- In a work-like environment, such as a simulated control room or flight deck;
- In a practical workshop with workbenches, word processors, or machines;
- On the job, under the supervision of a trainer, a skilled employee, or a supervisor.

Chapter 13 deals with supervised practice in all these locations except the last one; on-the-job training is covered in detail in Chapter 9.

There are a number of reasons for including practice sessions in training:

- They make it easier for learners to obtain feedback, both from performing the task itself and from the trainer or other learners.

- They are active and involving, and learners usually like practicing.
- They provide an opportunity for on-the-job application of concepts that are learned in the training setting.
- They can be structured in a variety of ways and can be used for different skills and training situations.
- They show whether competencies have been learned.

This chapter begins by looking at the stages that are typically involved in practical supervision. It then examines the psychology of practice in detail and suggests a number of ways in which practical learning can be encouraged. Finally, it explains why trainers should provide standard practical notes and describes a format for producing them.

Structuring Practice

Practice can be thought of as having two stages: the intermediate stage and the autonomous stage. During the intermediate stage, tasks are usually learned under the guidance of a trainer. A lot of the feedback that the learner receives initially comes from outside the task itself, for example, from a trainer's comments or from checking with an assessment guide or a sample finished product. This sort of feedback is called *extrinsic feedback*.

After repeated practice, learners start to rely less and less on extrinsic feedback. Instead, they gradually learn to respond to the "feel" of the task; the results of doing the task in certain ways, that is, the end product; and, in many computer-integrated systems, the cues and displays that the system itself provides. This sort of feedback is called *intrinsic feedback*. As learners began to rely on it, they enter the autonomous stage of learning a competency.

Figure 13.1. Stages of Learning a Competency

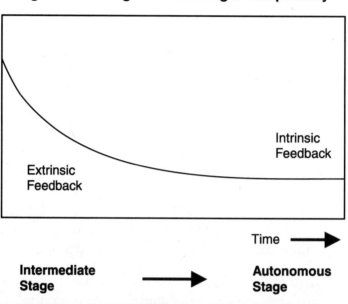

In a training program, there is no definite division between the two stages. Instead, the intermediate stage gradually gives way to the autonomous stage (Figure 13.1). However, the main features of each stage are discussed separately in this section for the sake of clarity.

Intermediate Stage

The trainer's goal during the intermediate stage is to help learners perform the task correctly to a reasonable standard of performance. During this stage the trainer does not need to worry too much about the finer points. What is more important is for learners to start to pick up the overall task sequence. In order to accomplish this goal the trainer should do the following:

- Ask learners to practice the whole competency area or a self-contained part of it. This approach is preferable to dividing the activity into small steps and practicing each separately.

- Encourage learners to be aware of the feel of the skill or task.

- Tell learners what tasks they will have to perform and the standard of work required. In addition to modeling the correct procedure during the demonstration phase, the trainer should provide written guidelines.

- Provide learners with a lot of practice time. Give learners the opportunity to practice performing the task several times in a row, preferably during the one training session. The trainer will need to know how to recognize when learners are becoming bored and tired and need a break.

- Move around the training room and correct any errors. The best way to help learners overcome errors is to demonstrate the task and then watch while they try it themselves.

- Explain what cues or signals are being acted on and any aspects of the procedure that need to be emphasized. The trainer should not worry too much about accuracy at this stage—it is more important that learners gain confidence in following the correct procedure.

- Take care not to embarrass or discourage learners who are making errors. Most people find it difficult to be told they are wrong so the trainer should emphasize how the task can be done better and encourage the learner's instead of focusing on what they are doing wrong.

- Encourage group learning. Many learners prefer to practice in groups. Try to encourage group learning if it is possible. An effective group provides support and a pooling of skills and work experiences.

Autonomous Stage

As learners gain confidence in performing a task, two things happen: First, they need less and less guidance from the instructor; secondly, they can concentrate more on speed, sequence, and accuracy. They gradually will learn to do the task automatically and easily even when working under pressure.

To support learners during the autonomous phase, the trainer should do the following:

- Demonstrate the finer points of the task, either to individual learners or to the group.

- Set new or higher standards for performing the task. These might include standards for preparation (for example, checking and diagnosing), process (the sequence in which the task is performed), and product (the size, shape and standard of the finished product).

- Observe learners closely while they are performing the task and correct any errors. By this stage, learners should be familiar with the tasks and should be able to concentrate on refining their levels of skill.

- Encourage learners to practice even after they can perform the task correctly. This encouragement is especially important when the task is seldom practiced in the workplace.

- Ensure that there is ongoing peer review and support. Learners are often very good at providing constructive criticism of on another's work and at helping one another apply and extend what they have been shown by the trainer.

- Supplement hands-on skills practice with exercises that help learners develop skills in systems understanding, teamwork, task planning, and anticipation of errors or problems. For example, learners might be asked to show on a diagram how the equipment that they are using is connected to a larger system or to respond, individually or as a small group, to a problem.

♦ Have learners do practical exercises that involve a mixture of unfamiliar tasks and familiar tasks.

Principles of Practical Instruction

Research into the psychology of learning suggests some important principles for supervising practical work:

♦ Make the environment as comfortable as possible;

♦ Be encouraging to learners;

♦ Let learners know what they have to do;

♦ Account for differences between individuals; and

♦ Provide guidance and feedback.

These principles and their applications are discussed briefly in the following section.

Make the Environment Pleasant

Learners are more likely to feel motivated if the physical environment is comfortable. Although many things about the physical environment, such as the size of a practical workshop or the availability of equipment linked to a larger system, may be outside the trainer's control, there are steps that can be taken to make sure that the physical environment is adequate.

These steps include ensuring that the following items are attended to:

- Windows, blinds, and fans are adjusted for comfortable ventilation and temperature;

- Sufficient tools or pieces of equipment are available and are in good working order;

- Lighting is adequate; and

- Plant noise or noise from other learners is not distracting the group. If it is too noisy, the trainer should try to find a quieter space or use a microphone and amplifier.

Be Encouraging

Learners, like anyone else, like to feel good about themselves and the things they can do. They are likely to feel great in situations that make them feel confident and worthwhile and to avoid situations that undermine their confidence.

For this reason, the trainer should not criticize their efforts in a manner that is likely to cause them emotional pain. The trainer can construct a supportive environment by doing the following:

- Avoiding comparing the work of different learners. For example, if the trainer likes to have a discussion at the end of an exercise, during which he or she comments on the learners' work, the trainer should not identify the learners. This lack of identification does not make what is said less valuable, but it does protect the learners. The trainer should also try to avoid comments like "most of you will find the next step to be very easy" for the same reason.

- Avoiding sarcasm. For example, quips like "I know you're trying, Helen, very trying" may seem clever to the other learners, but Helen may suffer a great deal of unnecessary hurt.

- Making positive comments to balance any criticisms wherever possible. No one's work is all bad, and the trainer needs to let learners know what they have done right as well as what errors they have made.

- Trying to help learners appreciate their own errors. For example, the trainer should ask them questions in order to help them discover their own mistakes rather than simply telling them.

- Thinking about how learners who show initiative or produce quality work can be rewarded. Rewards could include paying attention to someone, giving him or her the opportunity to learn a more advanced technique, or encouraging others to value his or her skill level. To understand the way rewards can be used effectively, the trainer should think about how poker machines work. Their reward systems are tangible and valued by players, are immediate, and are variable both over time and in terms of quantity of payout. The same principles can be applied for a more worthwhile purpose in practical training sessions.

Let Learners Know What Cues to Respond to

Practice will be more effective if learners know what the main cues for correct performance are so that they can monitor the way the task is done and can correct mistakes in the beginning. In the early stages of practice, the learners can learn obvious cues, such as the meaning of warning lights or the main operating parameters for computer-controlled processing. Many cues, however, are much more subtle than these. For example, the cues that an employee uses to assess the color or consistency of chemical substances such as paints or plastics are difficult to learn.

The trainer's long-term goal should be to help learners perform a competency without supervision. To act without supervision, they have to learn to respond to both subtle and obvious cues. The trainer can assist this process by doing the following:

- Commenting on the cues being acted on while demonstrating the task.

- Using extreme examples, such as a product with obvious flaws. The trainer can then gradually encourage learners to recognize less and less obvious flaws or product qualities.

- Watching out for cues that a number of learners are overlooking. In such a situation, the trainer should stop the learners and call them together so that the misunderstanding can be explained. For example, the trainer may give a new explanation or demonstrate a new example.

- Explaining how the task or skill will be assessed, so that learners understand the relative importance of each aspect of the task.

Cater for Individual Differences

Learners differ from one another in a number of ways that affect their ability to learn new skills or tasks:

- For any particular task, some learners will perform it better than other learners because of their different work experiences.

- Some learners have more aptitude for learning a given task than others. As discussed in Chapter 2, routine tasks are very dependent on under-the-surface skills. In any group, the learners may appear to have similar abilities, but if some are more skilled in these less visible areas, then they will learn more quickly.

- Learners vary in terms of the type of learning environments that they prefer. For example, some learners work better in a team, whereas others prefer to work on their own. Similarly, some like to innovate, whereas others prefer to follow.

The trainer will need to make allowances for the differences between learners by doing the following:

- Organizing practical instruction to cover routine skills and general principles before covering the specifics. For example, a series of sessions on using lathes could begin with an overview of their purposes, operating principles, and types of control mechanisms.

- Providing more difficult supplementary problems at the end of each exercise so that advanced learners do not finish quickly and become frustrated.

- Using competency guides, self-paced modules, or reference material to encourage learners to work independently, thereby freeing the trainer to help slower learners.

- Building a feeling of support within the group and encouraging learners to help one another when they run into difficulties.

Provide Guidance and Feedback

Providing guidance consists of directing learners' initial practice so that the task is more likely to be done correctly. For example, guidance is being used when the trainer moves around the room while learners are practicing and he or she encourages them to follow the correct procedure. Guidance can be provided in a variety of ways: physically, visually, and verbally.

- Physical guidance involves restricting a learner's choices and movements in some way. For example, machine controls may be locked or covered during the early stages of learning.

- Visual guidance relies on visually drawing attention to movements or processes. In complex system diagrams, for example, beginning operators may be asked to use a highlighter pen to trace out a system and then to go out on the site and try to track the different material paths.

- Verbal guidance is often given in a training session that combines explanation with demonstration. Learners are told about the task and what they have to do. Later, when practicing the task, they are reminded what steps to concentrate on.

Feedback refers to any information that indicates whether or not a task is being done correctly. There are many examples in the workplace:

- The quality of a finished product;
- The functioning of a piece of equipment that an employee is trying to fix;
- A display on a computer screen that indicates whether a system is functioning within the normal operating parameters.

There has been a great deal of research into the best ways to provide guidance and feedback. The main principles that have emerged from this research and apply to skills training are as follows:

Emphasize relevant cues. When a learner begins to learn a new skill, such as typing or operating a new piece of equipment, the trainer may have a difficult time assessing whether tasks are being done correctly and, in particular, what feedback is relevant. There are many cues, such as sounds, appearance, and visual data, that can indicate how well a task is being done. The trainer should let learners know what these main cues are by doing the following:

- Exaggerate the most important cues. For example, in a class on welding, the difference between a correct and incorrect cutting flame might be emphasized on a chart or in a demonstration.
- Omit irrelevant cues during the early stages of learning. For example, the beginning typist normally learns one cluster of keys at a time and ignores the rest. Gradually,

more and more keys and combinations of keystrokes are learned.

- Show learners what they are trying to achieve. If learners clearly understand what outcomes are expected, then they can monitor their own practice. For example, if operators on a production line know what the product should look like after it leaves them, they can spot errors more quickly. A job aid that draws attention to common product and packaging faults can help considerably. Similarly, employees who are being trained in-house with the expectation that they will receive a pay increase once they have been assessed as competent must be told clearly what the assessment criteria are so that they know what to work toward.

- Provide plenty of extrinsic feedback when a skill is first being learned. Initially the trainer should be careful to let learners know whether or not they are using the right techniques. Providing extrinsic feedback is important in skills training. It can be done in a variety of ways:

    - Moving around the group and look out for errors.
    - Intervening when a learner is using the wrong technique and demonstrating the correct way to perform the task. However, the trainers should avoid doing the whole task for the learner. Once the error has been corrected, let the learner attempt the task again.

The importance of extrinsic feedback in the workplace is diminishing and gradually being replaced by intrinsic feedback. More and more computer-based systems incorporate intrinsic feedback as an integral part of performing the job. Once the learner is familiar with using the system, little additional extrinsic feedback is needed.

Preparing Practical Notes

When learners have to do a practical exercise, they are often given instruction sheets to guide them. Various terms are used for these sheets: *task sheets, job sheets,* or *practical notes.* The term *practical notes* is used in this book to cover the variety of different types of notes.

The trainer should provide practical notes for formal practical training sessions that would require learners to perform a specific task or process. Practical notes have a number of useful functions:

- They reduce the number of repeated instructions that the trainer needs to give.

- They supplement the demonstration lesson by systematically showing each step or stage of the task.

- They make it possible to conduct practice sessions in which different learners work on different exercises.

- They encourage learners to work independently and to begin learning to monitor their own performance.

- They serve as a useful reference to help learners review their work.

- They provide additional technical information to accompany the demonstration lesson.

- They help new group members or those who arrive late to catch up with others.

- They show how a practical exercise is to be assessed.

- They help learners appreciate the relative importance of each stage.

The format used for practical notes will vary, depending on what subject is being dealt with, whether the practice session deals with discrete tasks or continuous processes, and whether the session is related to individual pieces of equipment or integrated systems.

Bibliography

Davis, R. (1974). *Learning system design.* New York: McGraw Hill.

Stammers, R., & Patrick, J. (1975). *The psychology of training.* London: Methuen.

In an effective test, different assessors would use the same criteria

Assess Skills

Assessment is one of the most difficult aspects of skills training. Many recognize that present approaches to assessment need rethinking, and the experience of formal assessment in industry has been limited by union opposition and other factors. Technological change has also contributed to these difficulties—work in traditional areas like typing or plumbing is easier to assess than the competence of a word-processor operator or a technician in a computer-integrated manufacturing environment. As with many areas of training, competency assessment is relatively straightforward when one is dealing with tasks but much more difficult with competencies that depend heavily on under-the-surface skills such as problem solving or system monitoring.

To some extent, these sorts of difficulties need to be examined within each section of industry as new assessment procedures are developed. However, it is easier to face this challenge if one is armed with the right concepts and can build on the assessment ideas that are meaningful in this changed context.

This chapter looks at what is known about assessing work skills and competencies. It begins by examining two different purposes of assessment: grading learners (norm-referenced assessment) and comparing each learner's results with a fixed competency standard (criterion-referenced assessment). Chapter 14 then looks at the issue of test effectiveness and describes ways of maximizing validity and reliability. Finally, it discusses the stages in developing assessment materials, which are concerned with the following:

- Selecting a sample of competencies or skills;
- Developing a method of assessment; and
- Carrying out the assessment and deciding the results.

A word about assessment terminology is in order before these topics are addressed. In some industries, the word *test* is unpopular, probably because it is reminiscent of time-and-motion studies and similar approaches. Although this negative feeling is understandable, the word *test* is often used as an alternative for *assessment* in the vocational-education literature and that is how it is used in this chapter. The terms should not be cause for concern to employees, instead employees should concentrate on the use or abuse of testing methods.

Norm-Referenced and Criterion-Referenced Tests

Tests can be designed for two different purposes:

- To compare learners' results (a norm-referenced test); and
- To compare a learner's results with a set of fixed criteria (a criterion-referenced test).

A norm-referenced test is intended to compare the performance of individuals on a specific set of tasks. For example, a norm-referenced test might involve marking learners' work and then using these marks to do the following:

- Decide who passes and who fails by ranking learners and then allowing a fixed percentage, for example, 80 percent, pass;
- Decide who are the best learners in the group; or
- Give letter grades like A+ and B- or marks like 65 percent and 72 percent.

Criterion-referenced tests, in contrast, are used to determine whether a learner has a particular level of mastery. A learner's performance is assessed in terms of whether or not particular criteria have been achieved. For example, a criterion-referenced test for word-processor operators might indicate the competency to be demonstrated ("copy type from neat handwritten text"), the criterion for satisfactory performance ("operators are required to type an average of fifty words per minute with a maximum error rate of two errors per minute"), and perhaps the relevant conditions ("using an IBM word processor"). Instead of a mark or letter grade, the learner would receive a check mark alongside each competency that he or she could perform.

To distinguish between norm-referenced tests and criterion-referenced tests, an analogy will be made between an individual's skill in a certain competency area and steel balls (Figure 14.1). In this analogy, the size of the ball represents the amount of skill that the individual has. The first approach to skills testing, which corresponds to norm-referenced assessment, would be to weigh each steel ball and to rank the balls from lightest to heaviest. The second approach, which corresponds to criterion-referenced assessment, would be to filter all of the steel balls through a sieve. Balls over a certain size would be caught and all the rest would pass through. The outcome would be two groups of balls: those that meet or exceed the criterion (in this analogy, the mesh size) and those that do not meet the criterion.

Assess Skills

Figure 14.1. Examples of a Norm-Referenced Test and a Criterion-Referenced Test

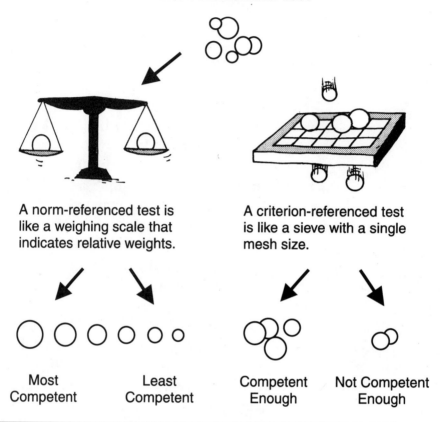

The main advantages of using norm-referenced tests are their popularity and convenience. Business encourages competitiveness, and many employers, administrators, and learners want to know how each individual's test score compares with those of his or her peers. This information is particularly important for recruitment and promotional purposes.

However, the marks that learners may receive in a norm-referenced test do not indicate much about what they know or what they can do. For example, a learner might have scored 78 percent on a test and have been ranked third in the group but this status does not indicate his or her level of competence. To determine competence, a criterion-referenced test is needed. Such a test indicates whether or not individual skills or competencies have been mastered to a specific level. The results of the criterion-referenced test make it easier for the trainer to decide who needs remedial work and what each learner has achieved during in-house training.

Characteristics of an Effective Competency Test

Each person has a mixture of skills in a given competency area. Some of these skills are routine and easily assessed whereas others are less visible. Chapter 2 detailed the different types of under-the-surface skills, and the importance of these less visible skills has been emphasized throughout this book.

Because one cannot peer inside a person and measure his or her skills directly, one can only estimate a person's skills and

Assessment is a Way of Estimating Skills

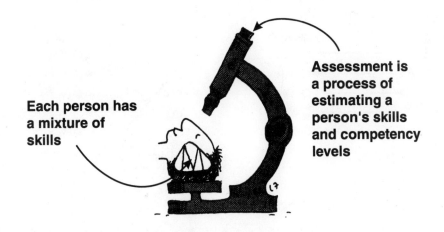

Each person has a mixture of skills

Assessment is a process of estimating a person's skills and competency levels competency levels indirectly. Such estimation is exactly what a competency test accomplishes.

A test's effectiveness refers to its ability to accurately estimate "real" skill levels. Ideally, a test's outcome corresponds exactly to a person's real skill levels. Figure 14.2 (a) shows this ideal relationship schematically for a test in a particular competency area.

Unfortunately, some tests do not work in this way. Unless care is taken with design and administration, a test may produce a result that is a poor indicator of a person's real ability. Figure 14.2 (b) illustrates a test that produces results that do not indicate a person's real skill levels. In this example, the person who is

Figure 14.2. Effective and Ineffective Tests

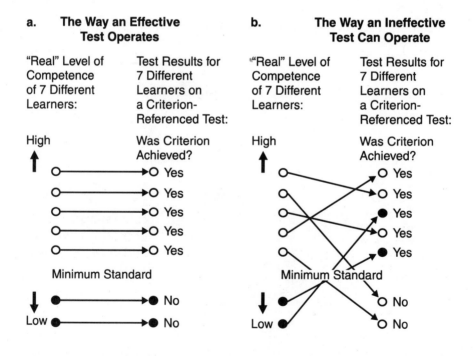

second-most competent failed to achieve the minimum standard. Inaccurate tests like this one can cause a lot of frustration among learners, especially if pay rates are linked to test results.

The diagrams shown in Figure 14.2 represent extremes. No test is completely effective or completely ineffective but all tests do not need to be designed so that the link between real skill levels and test outcomes are as close as possible.

The two most important measures of a test's effectiveness are validity and reliability. The following sections discuss these two measures and explain how to go about developing tests that are both valid and reliable.

Validity

The validity of a test is the extent to which it measures what it is supposed to measure. In a valid test, the test results correspond to the purpose of the test. Validity may be easier to understand in relation to the assessment of two sports: gymnastics and soccer. In gymnastics, assessment is based on points, and in soccer, assessment is based on goals. In each case, the assessment is a measure of how good the athlete or team is.

A "good" gymnast is someone who performs well. Because performance is what the scoring system measures and because each gymnast's routine is long enough to provide plenty of scope to demonstrate his or her ability, the gymnast's point system is very valid. A "good" soccer team, however, is one that plays well, and playing well includes more than scoring goals. For example, a team may use good teamwork and clever maneuvers but still fail to score because of a combination of bad luck and a strong opposition. In a situation like that, the team's score of zero would not be an accurate measure of its ability. Thus, scoring in soccer is not very valid.

In each of these examples, validity was based on seeing how well the test outcome (points, goals) corresponds to the competence of the athlete or team. An important point is that the term *validity* is only meaningful in relation to a particular purpose or context. A test that is a valid measure of skill in one particular industry or job area may not be valid in another.

The validity of a test can be gauged by asking the following three questions:

How representative are the skills covered by the test in relation to the tasks that people being tested will be required to do on the job? A valid test of a person's skills should assess a reasonable cross section of actual skills and not just focus on those that are easiest to test.

How well does the test distinguish between learners of different skill levels? If a test is valid, one would expect the learners who appear to be most skilled (as evidenced by practical exercises performed during class or reports from supervisors) to do well on the test. The trainer should make sure that the test discriminates between people of different skill levels. For example, if a criterion-referenced skill test indicates that group members with mixed abilities meet all the competency requirements, it may need to be revised.

How well does the test predict how individuals will perform on the job? If a test is valid, the results should correspond closely to the individual's real-life performance.

Reliability

Because the results of a competency test are only an estimate of a person's real skill level, the results will always be a little inaccurate. The reliability of a test is related to the absence of error in this estimating process. A reliable test is one that consistently estimates the person's real skill level, regardless of who administers it, which learners are tested, and who marks the test results.

To understand reliability better, consider the example from the previous section of scoring methods in gymnastics and soccer. In gymnastics, different judges often give different points for a routine; consequently, reliability in gymnastics is only medium to low. In soccer, however, there is rarely any disagreement between referees about whether a score has been made; consequently, scoring in soccer is very reliable.

The reliability of a test can be reduced by factors such as the following:

- Assessors who have not been properly briefed about what to look for;
- Assessment of a group of learners on the basis of different exercises;
- Unclear instructions for learners or assessors;
- Failure to have an adequate marking guide or checklist; and
- Test conditions or materials that vary from learner to learner.

The reliability of a competency test can be gauged by doing the following:

- Having several other instructors mark a cross section of learners' work, and comparing their marks with the trainer's; and
- Using the same test on learners twice. Different but equally difficult tasks or exercises could be substituted for the second trial. Subsequently, the results should be compared.

Whichever approach is chosen, the criterion for reliability is the same: the more similar the results, the more reliable the test.

The Process of Skills Assessments

The process of assessing a person's real skill level in a competency area can be divided into three phases:

- Selecting a sample of competencies or skills;
- Developing a method of assessment; and
- Carrying out the assessment and determining the results.

The development and administration of tests do not consist of these three clear phases, and this section is not intended to imply that they do. Indeed, if a trainer tries to devise an effective test of real workplace skills, he or she may find that the process is characterized by lack of clarity, at least during the developmental period.

The purpose of depicting assessment as a three-phase process is to illustrate a general sequence. What the trainer might actually need to do is to move backward and forward among the three phases until an assessment scheme has been developed that is effective enough to achieve its purpose. The next three sections look at each phase in turn.

Selecting a Sample of Competencies or Skills

Selecting assessment methods and combining them into a test that adequately deals with a competency area can be difficult. Two available options are to base the test on the following:

- The total competency; and
- A sample of skills.

These options are illustrated in Figure 14.3, and they are discussed briefly in relation to the two competencies shown in the figure.

Figure 14.3. Different Methods of Sampling Workplace Behaviors

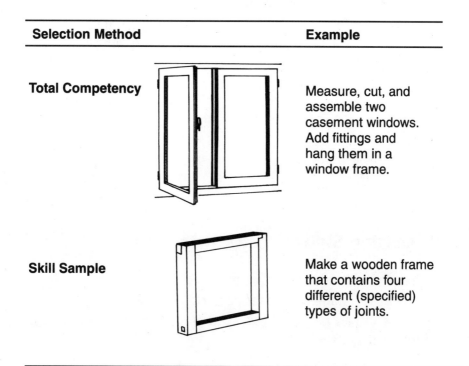

Selection Method	Example
Total Competency	Measure, cut, and assemble two casement windows. Add fittings and hang them in a window frame.
Skill Sample	Make a wooden frame that contains four different (specified) types of joints.

Total competency. This approach tests the whole competency under one particular set of circumstances. It is best suited to competencies that are self-contained and do not involve too much time to complete. For example, asking learners to make and hang a casement window during a workshop session may be realistic, but asking them to plan and determine the cost of a complex technical system may not be realistic.

Skill sample. In this type of assessment, learners have to perform a task or complete a project that does not correspond closely to what is done on the job, but does test a range of skills. For example, carpentry apprentices might demonstrate a range of joints in a workshop project. Engineering students might plan in detail how to make a component that has no industry applications but does involve a range of perceptual and drafting skills. The assumption behind such exercises is that because many skills apply equally well to a range of tasks, it makes sense to try to test the skills directly rather than concentrating solely on the specific ways they are applied in the workplace. Skill-sample tests are somewhat artificial and are best suited to general skills that have a variety of different applications.

To be effective, the activities chosen to represent the competency should cover a wide range of possible conditions, levels of difficulties and work processes. The bigger and more representative the sample of skills is, the better.

Assessing Skills and Knowledge

Tests can be divided into those that directly assess skills (sometimes called hand-on tests or performance tests) and those that assess knowledge, thinking, and understanding (sometimes called hands-off tests).

Testing Skills

Whenever possible, the trainer should try to test learners by having them demonstrate competencies (Figure 14.4). A competency test's goal is to duplicate working on the job.

During competency testing, the test conditions need to be carefully controlled to give each learner a fair and equal chance. Practical testing on integrated technical systems presents particular problems that need to be worked through. For example, in a problem-solving exercise, an electrical technician who makes the wrong decision early may subsequently not be able

Figure 14.4. Competency Test Characteristics

	Perform a Competency in a Real or Simulated Work Environment
Purpose	Assess Ability to Perform a Competency
Examples	• Complete a Routine Task • Operate a System • Rectify a Fault on a Simulator • Produce Something
Main Advantage	Provides Direct Evidence of Competence
Keys to Successful Use	• Well-Planned Exercises • Clear Guidelines for Learners • Accurate Rating Method • Time for Instructor to Set Up Tasks and Rate Performance
Potential Limitations	• Poor Sample of Behaviors • Inadequate Task Design • Poor Rating Procedure • Cost of Simulating Work Environment

to track down the problem. At the very least, a wrong decision can delay task completion beyond set time limits. Different decisions made early in a complex decision sequence can result in learners' being confronted with what is, in effect, a different test.

To some extent, the trainer has a choice between aiming for a realistic test over which he or she has little control (a test with low reliability) and a rigidly structured test that although reliable, might not be representative of real job requirements (a test with low validity). Ideally, a trainer should aim for both validity and reliability.

One way of balancing reliability and validity is to plan and assess a task in stages. For the problem-solving exercise just mentioned, the trainer could interrupt the procedure at a certain point if learners had made the wrong choice and put them back on track after recording the initial errors. This approach is not as bad as it might sound—in the workplace, a supervisor would be likely to do the same thing for an employee.

The trainer may want to conduct testing in the actual work environment, but there can be problems with doing so:

- Obtaining access to facilities in continuous processing and manufacturing industries or complex information systems is difficult;
- Some technical and information systems are particularly sensitive to access and interference;
- Machinery may be in short supply and constant use;
- A malfunction in other parts of a computer-integrated system may prevent or interrupt testing;
- Systems or equipment that are not related to the skills being tested may interfere with the test process; and
- Tests might damage equipment or processes, causing safety hazards.

For these reasons, a trainer may want to set up a simulated test environment. Examples currently used include mock-ups of bank-teller work stations, simulated food-production lines, flight simulators containing a complete flight deck, and operator consoles in power stations. Each of these environments would be linked to computer software designed to simulate typical workplace situations and problems.

Testing Knowledge

As Figure 14.5 indicates, the most common ways of testing knowledge are as follows:

Figure 14.5. Knowledge Test Characteristics

	Provide Written Answers	Method Answer Questions Verbally	Complete Ojective Test Items
Examples	• Write an Explanation • Give Reasons for a Particular Outcome	• Answer Probing Questions About How One Might React in a Particular Situation • Explain Why a Task Was Done a Certain Way	• Complete Fill-In Items, Multiple-Choice or True/False • Label a Diagram • Indicate Defects on a Photo or Sample of a Faulty Product
Main Advantage	Checks understanding of principles and of complex processes and systems.	Checks understanding during training or assessment. Allows gaps in knowledge to be explored.	Efficient way of testing a lot of information. Easy to standardize.
Keys to Successful Use	• Well-Planned Exercises • Preparation of Marking Guides • Time for Instructor to Read and Mark Answers	• Clear Questions • Standard Question and Probing Sequence • Adequate Response Time for Learners	• Meaningful Test Items • Instructor Skill at Item Writing • Time to Prepare and Validate Test Items
Potential Limitations	• Too Dependent on Language Skills • Difficult to Score	• Poorly Phrased Questions • Learners' Verbal Ability • Too Few Questions • Too Time Consuming for Instructor	• Poorly Written Items • Over-Concentration on Easy-to-Test Areas • Overemphasis on Facts Rather than Thinking

Assess Skills

- Tests that consist of questions and require written answers;
- Verbal tests, in which the trainer asks each learner a series of questions; and
- Objective tests consisting of standardized items such as multiple-choice or true-or-false questions.

There are several reasons for using approaches such as these to assess competence. First, they are often more convenient and cheaper than performance tests. They provide an effective way of standardizing assessment across large groups of learners, which is particularly important. Second, these sorts of approaches are a good way of checking understanding when used with performance testing. Learners might be observed demonstrating a competency and then quizzed verbally to make sure they really understand what they are doing.

Consider, for example, how a trainer would assess the skills of a power-station operator. A test using a simulated control program on a mock-up console might involve an "emergency" that the operator is required to respond to while being observed. It is possible that the operator might be lucky enough to pinpoint the faulty system or component immediately without any idea of what the real problem is or its causes are. The trainer could ask some probing questions to discover the knowledge and thinking behind the observable behavior.

Deciding Assessment Results

In planning skills assessment, the trainer needs to think carefully about the type of assessment results that are needed and the way they will be obtained. Obtaining assessment results involves the following:

- Planning a rating method;

- Deciding who is going to rate skill levels;
- Sorting out what to assess;
- Developing a way of recording results; and
- Trying out the assessment approach.

Plan a Rating Method

Tests can be designed for two different purposes: to compare learners' results (the norm-referenced approach) or to check whether a learner has achieved a competency standard (the criterion-referenced approach). Each of these approaches implies different ways of rating performance (Figure 14.6).

There also are other options. First, the trainer can norm-referenced and criterion-referenced ratings. Competencies can be divided into those that need to be performed to a specified level (criterion referenced) and those that involve more general skills (norm referenced). Second, criterion-referenced tests can be used with graded criteria such as the following:

4: Is skilled—can perform this task with no supervision.

Figure 14.6. Norm-Referenced and Criterion-Referenced Ratings

Typical Norm-Referenced Ratings			Typical Criterion-Referenced Ratings	
Exercise	Mark (%)	Position in Group	Task or Skill	Satisfactory?
Running	88	2	Typing	✓
Running	85	7	Filing	✓
Running	75	9	Bookkeeping	X

Assess Skills

3: Is skilled, but requires some supervision.
2: Has some skill, but requires supervision.
1: Is unable to perform this task.

In terms of the earlier analogy of the sieve and the steel balls, this approach is like using several layers of mesh to separate learners who can demonstrate different levels of competence (Figure 14.7).

Figure 14.7. Using Graded Assessment Criteria

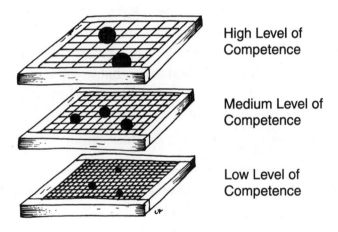

High Level of Competence

Medium Level of Competence

Low Level of Competence

Decide Who Is Going to Rate Skill Levels

Context is the main factor that determines who rates performance. An assessment is usually done by the trainer. In industry, an engineer, a supervisor or an experienced employee could do an assessment. In some situations, learners could assess themselves or their peers could do the assessment. Following are other factors that influence who assesses:

- Levels of experience. For example, because trainers' technical backgrounds vary, so do abilities to do the assessing.

- The degree of accuracy needed. For example, peer assessment can be adequate (and has the added benefit of being cost-effective) if it is only necessary to gauge progress.

A trainer does not have to decide on one option only. Figure 14.8 shows how different assessment methods can be combined. This example combines formal classroom testing, self-directed learning and self-assessment, field experience with completion of a skills logbook, and formal competency testing. The latter might be done by a committee of skilled employees and other technical experts, such as engineers.

Sorting Out What to Assess

Most assessments of skills or competencies are based either on a product that a learner procedures or the procedure by which a task is completed. These two options are discussed separately in this section.

Product assessment is usually associated with something directly produced at work or in a classroom. For example, it might involve the assessment of a plastic toy, a typed document, a steel fitting, or a consumer product. It might also include assessment of a report on practical experiments done in a laboratory or of an assignment demonstrating what was learned on an industry visit.

Process assessment focuses on the way a task is done. Process is typically assessed directly by observation using variables such as these:

- Accuracy of work;

- Use of correct process-monitoring sequences;

Figure 14.8. In-House Training and Assessment for a Competency Area

This diagram illustrates one of the many ways of combining different training and assessement approaches that deal with one competency area within an organization.

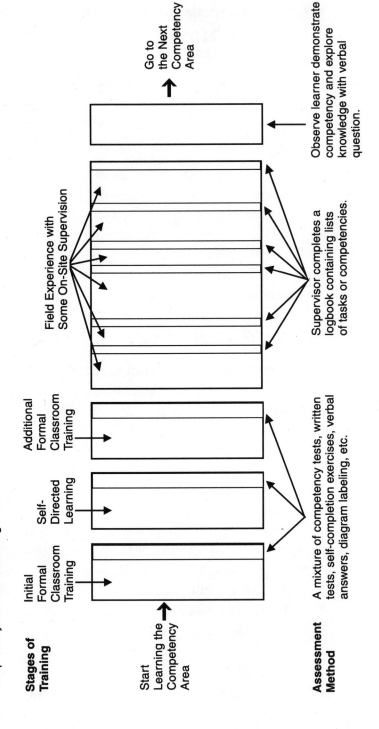

254 ◆   *Skills Training for Tomorrow's Workforce*

- How systematically the work is done;
- Attitude toward work, as evidenced by cleanliness, care, and persistence;
- Use of safe procedures;
- Degree of physical dexterity; and
- Speed of doing each stage of a task.

Develop a Way of Recording Results

The three most common ways of recording test results are as follows:

- Checklists that indicate what should be done when a person demonstrates a competency. Competency guides, which were discussed in Chapter 4, are very useful for this purpose.
- Rating scales for procedures that list the main aspects of doing the task well and are set out so that each aspect can be rated.
- Marking scales for assessing products. Designing marking scales for individual products is relatively easy. Once objective standards have been developed, the finished product can be compared to them.

The trouble with assessing each part of a task separately is that the sum of the parts may not add up to an accurate overall measure of competence, partly because it is often impossible to accurately weigh each aspect in terms of how much it contributes to overall competence. An alternative and equally respectable approach is for experienced employees or trainers to give an overall rating of the whole task or competency.

The only danger in an approach like this alternative is that because the assessment criteria are not specific, ratings may vary from assessor to assessor. Consequently, it is a good idea to accompany overall ratings with reliability checks, which might include having two or more people doing the assessing and having the assessors attend regular meetings to discuss the criteria they are using.

Run a Pilot Test on the Assessment Approach

By this stage, the trainer will have started to assemble a package of assessment materials, such as checklists and marking scales. The trainer should run a pilot test on the newly developed assessment package before using it widely. To prepare for the pilot test, the trainer should do the following:

- Write instructions for both learners and assessors. The instructions for the assessment package should be clear, complete, and easy to understand.
- Set the whole assessment package aside for a few days. Problems are easier to spot after some time away from the task.
- Think again about the validity and reliability of the test. Does it seem to measure what it is supposed to? Are instructions clear and realistic?
- Get the necessary equipment ready and, if appropriate, arrange access to a plant or a workshop.
- Meet with the people doing the skills assessment and brief them on their role.
- Try out the package and have someone observe the results.

List the things that need to be observed during the trial run (Figure 14.9). Then, meet again with observers and those involved in doing the assessment. Discuss how the test went, and think about how the assessment materials could be improved.

Figure 14.9. Checklist for Determining the Effectiveness of an Assessment Package

- [ ] Are instructions clear? (Get learners to repeat them in their own words to see if they really understand.)
- [ ] Did learners ask questions? (Written instructions can be prepared for questions that are often asked.)
- [ ] Were there any accidents or injuries? What changes need to be made to avoid them?
- [ ] Did the test seem to be measuring the skills it was intended to measure?
- [ ] Was there any damage to tools or equipment? What changes need to be made to avoid damage?
- [ ] Were there enough test materials and supplies?
- [ ] How long did it take to do the test?
- [ ] After testing each learner, were there any problems in getting things ready to test the next person?
- [ ] Did anything happen that could lower the validity or realiability of the results?
- [ ] Did assessors make any errors? Did they give away the correct procedure unfairly, or did they confuse learners by their approach?

Bibliography

Campbell, C., & Armstrong, R. (1988). A methodology for testing job task performance (Part 1). *JEIT, 12*(1).

Campbell, C., & Armstrong, R. (1988). A methodology for testing job task performance (Part 2). *JEIT, 12*(4).

Denova, C. (1979). *Test construction for training evaluation.* New York: Van Nostrand Reinhold.

Harris, D., & Bell, C. (1986). *Evaluating and assessing for learning.* London: Kogan Page.

Jones, A., & Whittaker, P. (1975). *Testing industrial skills.* New York: John Wiley & Sons.

Stiggins, R. (1987, Fall). Design and development of performance assessments. *Educational measurement: Issues and practice.*

Sullivan, R., & Elenburg, M. (1988, November). Performance testing. *Training & Development Journal.*

Wolf, A., & Silver, R. (1986). *Work-based learning: Trainee assessment by supervisors* (Report No. 33). Sheffield, UK: Manpower Services Commission.

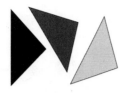

Index

A

Above-the-surface skills, 34-35
Action research, 67-69
Actual sequence, 132-133
Adult learning, 205-210
Assessment (or testing)
   competency samples, 244-246
   criterion-referenced tests, 236-239
   norm-referenced tests, 236-239
   of knowledge, 248-250
   of skills, 246-248
   pilot test, 256
   rating methods, 251-257
   reliability, 242-243
   results, 250-251, 255-256
   test characteristics, 239-243
   validity, 241-242, 255-256
Autonomous stage, 220, 223-224

B

Broad-based modules, 191

C

Clarity (how to achieve), 209-210

Collecting occupational data, 61-62
Communication skills, 19
Competencies
   assessing, 235-258
   competency areas, 29, 31
   competency samples, 244-246
   definition, 31-32
   editing competency lists, 92
   meaning of competence in a particular study, 88-89
   validation of competencies, 92
   ways of grouping competencies, 93
Competency guides
   definition, 74-76
   format, 75
Competency patterns, how to analyze, 134-136
Competency profile
   definition, 90, 134
   how to develop, 88-94
   using the profile to structure training, 134-136
Competency samples, 244-246
Competency-based training
   advantages and limitations, 86-87
   characteristics, 81-85
   how to set up, 88-94
Complex (computer-integrated) systems, 137-138
Computer simulation, 141-142
Computer-aided design/manufacture (CAD/CAM), 9
Computer-aided learning
   drill and practice, 167-168
   simulation, 169-170
   tutorials, 168-169
   uses and applications, 164-170
Computer-integrated manufacture (CIM), 9
Computer-integrated systems, 9-10
   training for, 137-138

Computer-managed learning, 170-173, 195
Computers in training
   computers and interactive video, 180-184
   cost issues, 176-178
   instructor issues, 178-179
   learner issues, 175-176
   merits, 173-179
   organizational issues, 174
   overview, 163-164
   resistance to, 184-186
   terminology, 164-165
Conceptual skills, 17
Conditions (in performance objectives), 100
Continuous (or interspersed) practice, 133-134, 222
Creative problem-solving skills, 17-18
Criterion-referenced assessment, 83, 85
Criterion-referenced tests, 236-239
Cross-skilling, 42

D

Demarcation barriers, 12, 56
Demonstrations
   and adult learning, 168-210
   conducting, 212-215
   demonstrating a task, 151-155, 203-217
   how to combine with explanation, 204-205
   how to combine with practice, 130-134
   lesson plan, 215-216
   preparing for, 210-212, 215-216
Descriptive survey research, 69-72
De-skilling, 15
Detailed task analysis, 76-77
Discrimination (how to train), 128-129
Drill and practice (using computers), 167-168

E

Encouragement, 225-226
Environment of learning, 213, 224-225
Equal access (to training), 55-56
Estimating skill levels, 239-241
Exploratory studies (how to conduct), 62-65
External labor market strategies, 54-55
External training, 139
Extrinsic feedback, 220, 231

F

Fault diagnosis and rectification skills, 19-20
Feedback, 85, 229
   extrinsic, 220, 231
   how to provide, 229-231
   intrinsic, 220, 231
Flexible manufacturing systems (FMS), 8
Ford, Professor Bill, 5-7, 15

G

Guidance, 229-231

H

Help screens, 120
Holistic thinking skills, 18

I

Immigrant employees, 22-23
In-house (formal) training, 140-141
In-house assessment, 49
Individualized learning

and competency-based training, 85
  catering to individual differences, 227-229
Industrial relations, 7
  and technoculture, 51
Industry analysis studies, 61-62
Information management skills, 18-19
Integrated training solutions, 56
Interactive video
  applications, 181-182
  meaning, 180
Intermediate stage, 221-222
Internal labor market strategies, 54-55
Interpersonal skills, 41
Interspersed (or continuous) practice, 133-134, 222
Intrinsic feedback, 220, 231

J

Job aids
  definition, 107
  types, 108
Job reference guides
  examples, 107-109
  how to prepare, 110-112
  types, 109-110
Jobs (definition), 28

K

Knowledge testing, 248-250

L

Labor market analysis studies, 61-62
Labor market strategies, 54-55
Learner guides

format, 196-199
meaning, 196-199
Learning
active nature of, 52-54
as navigation, 53
environment, 224-225
learning skills, 39-41
Lesson planning, 215-216
body, 214-215
conclusion, 215
introduction, 213-214
Levels of program structure, 125-127
Literacy skills, 18, 194

M

Meaningfulness (of learning), 206
Menus (in a computer system), 108
Modeling (in training), 207-208
Modified sequence, 132-133
Modular programs
and self-pacing, 193-195
how to introduce, 200-201
meaning, 189-193
role of learners, 193-195
role of trainers, 195-196
Modules
broad-based modules, 191-193
bridging, 207
in training, 190
Multiskilling, 43-44

N

Native employees, 22-23

Needs analysis, 65-67
   in conjunction with new technology, 66
Norm-referenced tests, 236-239
Novelty (in training), 208-209

O

Objectives, *see* Performance objectives
Occasional trainers, 158-159
Occupational analysis studies, 62
Off-site training, 139-140
On-line job aids
   examples, 108, 121
   types, 108, 120
On-the-job learning, 48-49, 142-143
   contact with the learner, 150-151
   demonstrating a task, 151-155
   how to conduct, 148-149
   planning, 149-150
   types, 147-148

P

Part learning, 130-132
Performance objectives
   and competencies, 83
   format, 97-101
   hints for writing, 103-105
   uses and limitations, 101-102
Practice
   autonomous stage, 223-224
   continuous, 133-134
   extrinsic feedback, 220
   how to combine with demonstrations, 130-132
   intermediate stage, 221-222

    intrinsic feedback, 220
    spaced, 133-134
    structuring practice, 220-221
    supervising on-the-job practice, 155
Prerequisites (of learning), 206-207
Procedural cues (in a computer system), 120

R

Rating skills, 251-253
Reliability, 242-243
Research approaches, 60-61
Roles (of trainers), 47-57

S

Self-assessment, 198-199
Self-directed learning skills, 18
Self-management skills, 17
Self-paced learning
   and learners, 193-195
   and trainers, 195-196
   in modular training, 191-196
Senses (how to use), 208-209
Sequences of steps (how to train), 128
Simple task analysis, 74-76
Simulation (using computers), 141-142, 169-170
Skill formation, 5, 13-16, 44
Skill-related career paths, 7
Skill sample assessment, 244-246
Skills
   cognitive, perceptual, psychomotor skills, 14
   influences of new technology, 7-10, 52
Skills assessment, *see* Assessment

Skills audit, *see also* Competency profile
   analyzing training needs, 65-67
   conducting an exploratory study, 62-65
   developing a competency profile, 88-94
   simple task analysis, 74-76
   types of workplace research, 60-61
Skills iceberg model, 35-41
Skills in short supply, 16-20
Skills testing, 246-248
Social context (of skills), 20
Spaced practice, 133-134
Standards (in performance objectives), 100-101
Structuring training, 125-145

T

Task analysis
   detailed task analysis, 76-77
   simple task analysis, 74-76
Task management skills, 36-38
Task skills, 33-36
Tasks (definition), 32
Taylor, Frederick, 10, 77
Teamwork skills, 19
Technical user manuals, 112
   examples, 108
   how to structure, 115
   importance of, 112
   indexing, 118
   page formats, 116
   steps in producing, 114-118
Technoculture, 5-7, 51
Technology, 7-10
   and work organization, 52
   blurring of boundaries, 56

Test characteristics, 239-243
Testing, *see* Assessment
Total competency assessment, 244-246
Trade classifications, 22
Training cues, 128, 226-227
Training needs analysis, 65-67
　research methods, 72-74
Training networks (in the organization), 158
Transfer of skills, 143-144, 155-157
Tutorials, 168-169

U

Under-the-surface skills, 27-28
　training in, 49-51
Up-skilling (definition), 42
User manuals, *see* Technical user manuals

V

Validity, 241-242
Videodisc, *see* Interactive video

W

Wage and salary earners, 22
Whole (task) learning, 130-132
Women's skills, 21-22
Work organization
　and technoculture, 51
　overview, 10-13
　relationship to production, 12
Work relations
　and technological change, 16
　from control to commitment, 11

Work-environment skills, 38-39
Workplace learning
    encouraging a learning culture, 157-160
    skills needed, 39-41
Workplace research (types of), 60-61

- Editor: Pat Gonzalez
- Production Editor: Dawn Kilgore
- Interior Design and Page Composition: Judy Whalen
- Cover Design: Paul Bond

This book was edited and formatted using 486 PC platforms with 8MB RAM and high resolution, dual-page monitors. The copy was produced using Word-Perfect software; pages were composed with Corel Ventura Publisher software; and cover and art were produced with CorelDRAW software. The text is set in thirteen on fifteen Times, and the heads are set in Kabel Medium and Bold. Proof copies were printed on a 400-dpi laser printer and final camera-ready output on a 1200-dpi laser imagesetter by Pfeiffer & Company.